HOUSTON
classic
DESSERTS

HOUSTON *classic* DESSERTS

Recipes from Favorite Restaurants

ERIN HICKS MILLER

PELICAN PUBLISHING COMPANY
GRETNA 2010

ISBN 9781589808362
Text by Erin Hicks Miller
Edited by Erin Hicks Miller, Jeffrey Linthicum
Photography by William Jones Miller, Fulton Davenport
Artwork and Paintings by William Jones Miller
Production by William Jones Miller

Layout based on a design by Kit Wohl

Printed in China

Published by Pelican Publishing Company, Inc.
1000 Burmaster Street, Gretna, Louisiana 70053

For sweet Ava Jane Miller

Contents

CAKES

CUSTARDS & PUDDINGS

PIES & TARTS

COOKIES, ICE CREAM & CANDY

INTRODUCTION

> "SEIZE THE MOMENT. REMEMBER ALL OF THOSE WOMEN ON THE TITANIC WHO WAVED OFF THE DESSERT CART."
>
> *~ERMA BOMBECK*

I love to cook and I love to eat. I'm the girl at the gym on the cross-trainer watching Food Network - the one who's planning lunch while she's eating breakfast - the one who's always anxious to try out a new recipe. In fact, 'Piggy' is a term of endearment in my household.

I've had many journeys - the restaurant business, the medical supply industry, real estate, design, decorating, even a stint selling gemstones (I really enjoyed that one. I was draped in jewels from morning 'til night that Christmas!) But this journey would lead me to discover that being a cook is one thing - being a dessert maker and baker is something entirely different.

Baking is truly a science. There's no 'a pinch of this' and 'a splash of that'. This is a game of precision and you must really wrap your head around it to bake successfully. No fooling. I received professional instruction on some of the techniques – but I learned from the best so you don't have to. If you aren't exactly sure how to brown or clarify butter, look no further. Instruction awaits you inside this book.

Every recipe was tested and re-tested (and eaten) in my own kitchen (and the kitchen's of some very supportive friends) so that you can re-create anything in this collection of the most classic desserts ever assembled from Houston's iconic restaurants and bakeries.

Making dessert is much easier when following a few basic rules. Begin only when there are no other distractions. Read the recipe entirely. Read the recipe again. Gather *all* of the ingredients, avoiding substitutions. Locate the equipment you will need and (this is important) take the time to measure everything into separate containers before cooking anything. This procedure is referred to as preparing the 'mise en place'. The technique - and the phrase - is easy to remember if you think of it as having your 'mess in place'. Sound complicated? It isn't. Trust me on this one. It's very sad to discover that you're missing a key ingredient in the middle of cooking a recipe.

I hope you enjoy cooking from this book as much as I enjoyed putting it together. (Every recipe here is truly 'blow-your-skirt-up-good'). Sure, it would be easier to visit the fine restaurants and bakeries represented here (and I hope you do) than to slave over a hot oven, covered in sugar and flour. But the satisfaction of saying, "I made this," will make it taste even better.

I guarantee it.

- Erin Hicks Miller

CAKES

Cake is a bigger part of your life than you probably realize. Think about it. Think of the countless celebrations and momentus events in your life when a cake represented the acknowledgment of an achievement. Weddings, birthdays, anniversaries and holidays are celebrated around the world every day and, more often than not, there's a cake in the room to mark the occasion. History reveals that it's been that way for a looooong time.

Romans were the first to write about cake. In 8 A.D, the poet Ovid referred to his own birthday festivities as a day 'with party and cake.' Most likely this would have been a rudimentary, honey-sweetened version of what we enjoy today, but the components were the same: sugar, flour and eggs.

When making any of the cakes or tortes in this chapter, keep these useful tips in mind:

-An inexpensive oven thermometer from the grocery store is the best piece of baking equipment you can own.

-Dark pans or those with a dull or nonstick finish absorb more heat, causing a darker and thicker crust on your cake. Shiny pans reflect heat and usually result in a thinner crust.

-Sharply tap the cake pans once or twice on the counter after the batter is added. This helps remove air bubbles and makes the cake rise more evenly.

-Always check for doneness 5 to 10 minutes before the stated time in the recipe.

-Remember to open and close the oven door gently and keep it open for as little time as possible to keep heat loss to a minimum.

While other restaurateurs spend a lifetime 'getting it right', Michael Cordua manages to skillfully juggle the duties of Owner and Executive Chef at six award-winning, Houston-area restaurants. The only Texas chef ever inducted into Food & Wine's 'Hall of Fame', Cordua's reputation as a pioneer of South American cuisine has cemented him as a standout in the Latin American culinary movement.

Artista, Cordua's elegant creation at Houston's Hobby Center, is perfectly situated for 'dinner and a show'. Theatrically high ceilings and expansive walls of glass afford spectacular views of the downtown skyline and Tranquility Park.

CHOCOLATE GANACHE

12 ounces	semi-sweet chocolate, chopped
1½ cups	heavy whipping cream

Place chocolate in a double boiler over low heat.

In a saucepot, bring the heavy cream to a simmer and remove from heat.

Pour the warmed cream over the chocolate to slowly melt. Once chocolate is melted, slowly bring cream and chocolate together with a spatula or whisk.

Pour ganache over chocolate mousse layer and chill to set. Slice into 2-inch brownie shaped squares and serve.

ARTISTA
DELIRIO DE CHOCOLATE

Inspired by the Parisian Opera Cake, this decadent chocolate trifecta manages to be both light in texture and intense in flavor. Skip the coffee... got milk?

YIELD: 30 SERVINGS

CHOCOLATE TRUFFLE CAKE

1 cup	cake flour		½ cup	olive oil
1½ cups	sugar		¼ cup	sour cream
¼ cup	dark cocoa powder		1 cup	heavy whipping cream
2 teaspoons	baking soda			
½ cup	egg whites			

Preheat oven to 300°F.

In a large mixing bowl, sift together the flour, sugar, cocoa powder and baking soda.

In a separate bowl using a hand mixer or stand mixer, whisk egg whites and oil for 2 minutes.

Add dry ingredients in small batches until fully incorporated.

Add sour cream until fully incorporated.

Lastly, add whipping cream and mix for 4 minutes.

Spray one full-sized sheet pan with cooking spray and place parchment on top.

Spread cake batter evenly with spatula.

Bake for 40 minutes. Remove and cool on a cooling rack.

CHOCOLATE MOUSSE

16 ounces	semi-sweet chocolate, chopped		1 teaspoon	powdered gelatin
½ cup	unsalted butter		1½ cups	heavy whipping cream
5	egg yolks			
1 cup	superfine sugar			

In a double boiler melt the semi-sweet chocolate with butter.

Using a hand or stand mixer, whisk together egg yolk and sugar until ribbons form.

Temper chocolate with egg yolk; then combine remaining egg yolk.

In a small heat-proof bowl or metal measuring cup, combine the gelatin and a ¼ cup of the heavy cream. Let stand for 10 minutes. Stirring constantly, dissolve the gelatin and cream over medium heat. Add the softened gelatin to the chocolate mixture.

In a chilled bowl using a hand or stand mixer, beat remaining cream until medium peaks form. Temper chocolate with whipped cream; then gently fold in the remaining whipped cream.

Spread a ½-inch layer of mousse on top of cake. Chill cake and mousse for a minimum of 3 hours.

RDG + BAR ANNIE
CHOCOLATE COBBLER

These luscious cobblers are best made with Valrhona cocoa, a favorite brand among chefs. It costs a bit more, but the recipe requires very little and makes this oozy-centered cobbler unforgettable.

YIELD: SIX 6-OUNCE COBBLERS

CHOCOLATE SHORTBREAD

¼ cup	unsalted butter, softened	1 teaspoon	cocoa powder
¼ cup	powdered sugar	¼ teaspoon	salt
½ cup plus			
2 tablespoons	all-purpose flour		

Preheat oven to 350°F.

In a mixing bowl, combine all of the ingredients and blend well with a spoon to form a dough. Divide the dough between six foil cups (½ cup volume) or china ramekins and press to cover the bottom. Bake for 20 minutes. Remove from oven and allow to cool.

COCOA BISCUIT TOPPING

1 cup plus		¼ teaspoon	salt
2 tablespoons	all-purpose flour	1 teaspoon	baking powder
2 teaspoons	cocoa powder	2 tablespoons	unsalted butter
⅓ cup	granulated sugar	½ cup	heavy cream

In a mixing bowl, combine all of the dry ingredients. With your fingers, cut the butter into the dry ingredients to form a coarse meal. Stir in the cream to form a dough. Do not over mix. Refrigerate the mixture.

CHOCOLATE FILLING

½ cup	unsalted butter, melted	½ teaspoon	vanilla
¾ cup	granulated sugar	1	egg, extra large
¼ cup	cocoa powder	⅓ cup	all-purpose flour
¼ teaspoon	salt		

In a mixing bowl, combine the melted butter, sugar, cocoa powder, salt and vanilla and mix well. Add the egg and stir to incorporate. Add the flour and stir to combine. Refrigerate.

Preheat oven to 350°F.

Divide the chocolate filling between the cups lined with the baked short bread. Distribute the pecan cocoa nib mixture over the chocolate filling. Pinch the biscuit topping into thumb nail size pieces and layer over the pecan cocoa nib mixture.

Bake on a sheet pan for 25 minutes. The biscuit topping should be cooked but the interior should remain soft and gooey. Allow to cool for 15 to 20 minutes, then gently remove the cobblers from the foil cups or ramekins. The cobblers may be re-heated at serving time.

Serve with chocolate gelato or vanilla ice cream.

Cafe Annie was the 'queen' of Houston restaurants for many years. When she grew up, moved down the street and became RDG + Bar Annie, folks were thrilled that Chef and Owner Robert Del Grande kept many of the favorites from the Cafe Annie menu. The filet mignon crusted with ground coffee and their wonderful tortilla soup are among them.

A trifecta of awards has resulted- not only was RDG+Bar Annie named best new restaurant in Texas by Texas Monthly and one of the top ten new restaurants in America by Forbes, Del Grande is a 2010 James Beard Foundation Outstanding Chef semifinalist.

PECAN FILLING

¼ cup	cocoa nibs
¼ cup	pecans (lightly toasted)
1 tablespoon	granulated sugar

Combine all the ingredients in a food processor and blend to form a coarse meal.

Although Carrabba's restaurants can be found all over the United States these days, only two are still owned by the family.

Carrabba's is truly a family affair. The majority of the recipes came from Damian's mother and Johnny's grandmother, Grace Mandola. Straight from Italy, her recipes have been handed down for generations.

Dessert Rosa is Rose Mandola Carrabba's adaptation of a 'Better than Sex' cake published in the Houston Chronicle in the early 70's. There are more than 500 different recipes out there for this type of cake and as best she can recollect, the bananas and pudding are what make this recipe her own.

If you have ever had the opportunity to meet Mama Rose, you know she's quite a character. Is this cake really better than sex? Rose says we all know different!

CARRABBA'S
DESSERT ROSA

This delicious, moist, yellow butter cake is topped with pastry cream, bananas, strawberries, pineapple and whipped cream. If you are looking for a shortcut, a Duncan Hines butter cake mix can be substituted for the moist yellow cake recipe below.

YIELD: 12 SERVINGS

CAKE

3¾ cups	all-purpose flour		2½ cups	granulated sugar
2¼ teaspoons	baking powder		3	eggs
2½ teaspoons	baking soda		1½ teaspoons	vanilla extract
1 cup	unsalted butter		2½ cups	buttermilk

Preheat the oven to 350˚F.

Spray a 2 ½-inch deep 9-by-13-inch cake pan with bakers spray.

Sift together the flour, baking powder and baking soda. Set aside.

In a large bowl, cream together the butter and sugar until light and fluffy. Beat in the eggs, one at a time, then stir in the vanilla. Beat in the flour mixture alternately with the buttermilk, mixing just until incorporated.

Pour batter into prepared pan.

Bake for 30 to 35 minutes or until toothpick inserted in the middle comes out clean.

Let cake cool.

TOPPING

20 ounces	prepared sweetened crushed pineapple		4	bananas (¼-inch slices)
2 packages	frozen strawberries, sliced (20 ounces)		3 cups	instant vanilla pudding, prepared (1 package)
			8 ounces	cool whip

After cake has cooled, poke holes throughout cake with a skewer (4 across and 6 down) in order for the juices from the pineapple and strawberries to seep throughout the cake. Using a slotted spoon, spread pineapple over cake.

Again using a slotted spoon, lay strawberries then bananas over pineapple. Spread pudding over bananas. Using the back of a spoon, cover cake with cool whip and smooth the cool whip with the spatula making sure no pudding shows through cool whip. Cover cake with dome lid and refrigerate for 3 hours.

NOTE: Be sure to use a slotted spoon for the pineapple and strawberries. You want some of the juice from the fruit but not so much that the cake gets overly soggy.

MOCKINGBIRD BISTRO
Warm Bittersweet Chocolate Torte

This impressive and sexy dessert is surprisingly easy to create. You can make the mixture up to 4 hours in advance and refrigerate. The dark glow of the uber-chocolatey molten center mixed with raspberry puree is completely satisfying and utterly sinful.

YIELD: SIX 6-OUNCE COBBLERS

7 ounces	bittersweet chocolate	1¾ cups	powdered sugar
¾ cup plus 2 tablespoons	unsalted butter	4	eggs
1 cup	all-purpose flour	4	egg yolks

Preheat oven to 450°F.

Combine the chocolate and butter in a double boiler and melt over simmering water (do not let water touch the bottom of pan or bowl).

Sift the sugar and flour into a large mixing bowl.

In a separate bowl, beat the eggs and egg yolk.

Pour the warm chocolate mixture into the eggs.

Fold flour mixture into egg-chocolate mixture with a spatula.

Spoon mixture into six 4-inch aluminum pans. (I used silicone baking cups that worked wonderfully).

This can be refrigerated for 4 hours if you would like to make ahead.

Bake 7 to 9 minutes if mixture is at room temperature, or 10 to 12 minutes if mixture is cold, until centers are quite soft.

Invert each torte onto a plate and serve with vanilla sauce (creme anglaise) and raspberry sauce (pureed, sweetened raspberries).

Garnish with fresh berries, if desired.

Executive Chef and Owner John Sheely spent most of his cooking career in high-end restaurants, but a casual concept restaurant had been mulling around in his head for a long time. A 'comfy hangout' where guests can enjoy a glass of wine and partake of comfort-type food, Mockingbird Bistro Wine Bar is the realization of that inspired idea.

The upscale-yet-casual atmosphere has 'gothic' leanings due to the unique metal light fixtures which originally hung in one of Houston's first upscale eateries, Sonny Look's.

The fare here combines Sheely's Texas roots with traditional techniques - a 'country-French-meets-American-market' menu that has garnered rave reviews from diners and critics alike. Sheely updates the menu seasonally to take advantage of the ingredients available at market, as well as to give him the freedom to exercise his creativity.

KENNY & ZIGGY'S
NEW YORK CHEESECAKE

Chef Ziggy Gruber personally promises that this is, "the greatest cheesecake in the history of cheesecakes." Made originally by Ziggy's grandfather Max at the Famous Dairy Restaurant in Brooklyn and later at the famed Rialto Deli on Broadway in Manhattan, this creamy confection has been a favorite for generations.

YIELD: 9-INCH CAKE

1 cup plus 3 tablespoons	all-purpose flour	½ cup	unsalted butter, softened (4 ounces)
2 cups	granulated sugar	5 packages	cream cheese, softened (2½ pounds)
2½ teaspoons	lemon zest, grated	1½ teaspoons	orange zest
½ teaspoon	vanilla	5	eggs
3	egg yolks	¼ cup	whipping cream

Preheat oven to 400°F.

Butter the sides and bottom of a 9-inch springform pan.

In a bowl, combine 1 cup of the flour with ¼ cup of the sugar, 1 teaspoon of the lemon zest and ¼ teaspoon of the vanilla. Form a well in the center and add one egg yolk and all of the butter. Work with a fork to make a dough. Add up to 2 tablespoons of water, if necessary, to make a pliable dough. Form into a ball, cover with plastic wrap and refrigerate for one hour.

In the bowl of a mixer, combine the cream cheese, the remaining 1¾ cups sugar, 3 tablespoons of flour, 1½ teaspoons lemon zest and all of the orange zest and beat until smooth. Add the 5 whole eggs, the remaining 2 egg yolks and the remaining ¼ teaspoon of vanilla and beat well. Add the heavy cream and beat again.

Roll out one-third of the chilled dough on a floured surface; the dough will be very moist and fragile. Roll it out in pieces and evenly press them, with your hands, into the bottom of the prepared pan. Don't worry if it looks like it is going to fall apart. Bake until golden, about 15 minutes, and cool in the pan on a wire rack.

Increase the oven temperature to 500°F.

Roll out the remaining dough in pieces and evenly shape them to fit the sides of the pan, a piece at a time. Make sure there are no holes in the crust and try to keep the edges neat.

Pour the cream cheese mixture into the crust. Bake for 10 to 12 minutes.

Reduce the heat to 200°F and continue baking for 1 hour.

Turn off the heat and keep the oven door open wide. Let the cake cool in the oven for 30 minutes..

Remove from oven and cool in pan on a wire rack for 30 minutes. Run a spatula along the side of cheesecake to loosen. Refrigerate uncovered for 3 hours or until chilled. Cover and continue to refrigerate until ready to serve.

Top the cake with fresh strawberries and pre-packaged strawberry glaze.

DACAPO'S
FRESH PEAR BUNDT CAKE

A Dacapo's customer favorite, this decadent, old-fashioned, pear and spice cake is drizzled with a creamy vanilla icing and topped with chopped pistachios. Make sure the pears are firm and not overripe. Pears that are too ripe will cause the batter to be runny and the cake will be much too heavy.

YIELD: 8 TO 12 SERVINGS

CAKE

3 cups	flour		1 tablespoon	baking soda
2 cups	granulated sugar		1 tablespoon	cinnamon
1 cup	vegetable oil		1 teaspoons	salt
3	eggs		3 cups	ripe pears, chopped
1 tablespoon	vanilla		¼ cup	pistachios, chopped

Preheat oven to 350°F.

In a bowl, combine the flour, baking soda, cinnamon and salt. Set aside.

In a stand mixer or with a hand mixer, cream the eggs and the sugar. Add the vanilla and then slowly add the oil, mixing well.

Add the flour mixture to the bowl, about a half cup at a time and mix well.

Add the pears and stir to combine.

Pour into a well greased bundt pan.

Bake for 1 hour or until a toothpick inserted in the cake comes out clean.

ICING

1 cup	powdered sugar		2 tablespoons	half-and-half
½ teaspoon	vanilla		1 tablespoon	orange juice

In a small bowl, combine all the ingredients and stir slowly to form a creamy icing.

Spread or drizzle over cake. Immediately sprinkle fine chopped pistachios over the wet icing.

NOTE: Christy Breining substituted Grand Marnier for the orange juice in her icing and said it was great!

Sometimes a really great bakery also manages to squeeze in a savory menu that lives up to its cookies, cakes and pies. Dacapo's is one of those bakeries. The salads, soups, sandwiches, and sides here are captivating enough to garner a lunchtime crowd that resembles the running of the bulls. The Houston Press even awarded their B.L.T. top sandwich honors. Savories aside, people come here for the sweets. The Banana Split Cake is out of this world as are their Italian Creme and Red Velvet cakes.

The Biggerstaff sisters opened Dacapo's 15 years ago, following a family tradition started by their grandfather who owned a bakery in the 1920's in Dewey, Oklahoma. Dacapo is an Italian musical term that literally means 'to begin again' - which they have done in the heart of Houston's Heights area to critical acclaim.

Textile is notably ensconced in Houston's ninth oldest building, which once served as an oriental textile mill. The interior is laced with wonderful fabrics and textures - making the industrial atmosphere interesting and intimate. But even more intimate are the dessert tastings in the kitchen on Tuesdays, when the restaurant is closed.

Plinio Sandalio, the avant garde Pastry Chef of Textile, welcomes up to 12 people into the kitchen every Tuesday for a tasting menu like no other. When we visited, the savory part of our tasting menu began with Sweet Potato Beignets drizzled with honey and served with... get this... Bacon-Flavored Ice Cream! Sweet desserts included a Pear Tart with Salted Caramel Ice Cream and Blue Cheese and the wonderful almond cake featured here. Each was as amazing as it was unusual.

TEXTILE
ALMOND CAKE WITH CARAMELIZED FIGS

This is an easy and uncomplicated dessert, adapted from a recipe by David Lebovitz.

The temperature and texture contrasts make eating it really fun, especially when the succulent fig seeds pop in your mouth.

YIELD: 24 SERVINGS

CAKE

¾ cup	almond paste		6	eggs, (room temperature)
1¼ cups	granulated sugar			
1 cup plus 2 tablespoons	unsalted butter, softened (10 ounces)		1¼ cups	all-purpose flour
			1½ teaspoons	baking powder

Preheat oven to 350°F.

Using a stand mixer with paddle attachment, combine the almond paste and the sugar. Whip on low until the almond paste and sugar mixture resembles cornmeal.

Add the butter and mix on medium speed for 2 minutes. Scrape the sides of bowl and mix for another 2 minutes.

Add the eggs and whip on medium high for 2 minutes. Scrape the sides of bowl and whip for another 3 minutes.

In separate bowl, combine flour and baking powder and add to mixer, whipping for 1 minute.

Spread almond cake batter into greased 9-by-13-inch pan.

Bake for 25 to 30 minutes, or until golden brown.

CARAMELIZED FIGS

½ cup	granulated sugar		1	cinnamon stick
1 cup	light brown sugar		10	dried Turkish figs, quartered
2 cups	water			

In a medium pot over high heat, melt granulated sugar and ½ cup of the light brown sugar. Continuously whisk sugar until dissolved to prevent burning.

Cook until golden brown in color, remove from heat.

Slowly add water while whisking. Add the remaining sugar, cinnamon and figs. Stir to combine.

Simmer over low heat for 10 minutes.

To serve, simply toast almond cake in oven. Serve cake with warm figs and vanilla ice cream.

REEF
CRÈME FRÂICHE CHEESECAKE

This is some of the best cheesecake we have ever had. The crème frâiche makes it uniquely creamy and gives it a lovely tang. You *may* substitute sour cream for the crème frâiche... but don't.

YIELD: SIX 6-OUNCE CAKES

FILLING

15 ounces	cream cheese, softened		2	eggs
¾ cup plus			1	egg yolk
2 tablespoons	granulated sugar		2 tablespoons	milk
½	vanilla bean, split lengthwise, scraped		18 ounces	crème fraiche

Using a stand mixer with paddle attachment, combine the cream cheese, sugar and the vanilla bean on low until smooth, scraping constantly.

Add the eggs, the yolk and milk and mix well. Last, fold in the crème frâiche to combine.

CRUST

4½ ounces	graham cracker crumbs		6 tablespoons	unsalted butter, melted
1	egg		½ tablespoon	cinnamon
1½ tablespoons	sugar			

Preheat oven to 350˚F.

Put graham cracker crumbs in food processor, add the sugar and pulse. Then add the butter and cinammon. Place six 3-inch metal baking rings on a sheet pan lined with parchment paper. (I used an extra large muffin tin with push-up bottoms). Press crust into bottom of metal baking rings about ¼-inch high. Place in oven and lightly toast, approximately 8 minutes. Remove and cool.

Preheat convection oven to 250˚F; regular oven to 300˚F.

Scoop cheesecake mixture into the molds ¼-inch from the top.

Bake for 20 minutes on convection. Turn off convection. Turn on regular oven and bake for an additional 20 minutes, rotating frequently. (If you are baking in a regular oven only, bake for 40 to 50 minutes, rotating frequently).

Cool to room temperature. Use blow torch to warm mold then remove ring.

POACHED DRIED SOUR CHERRIES

1½ cup	dried sour cherries		3 tablespoons	water
½ cup	red wine		1	vanilla bean, split lengthwise, scraped

Bring to a boil and boil for 1 full minute to cook out alcohol. Cool at room temperature.

Clever flavor profiles and a savviness for seafood are the calling card of Chef Bryan Caswell, who owns Reef with Co-founder Bill Floyd. Houston-born Caswell grew up fishing in the Gulf Coast waters and successfully marries his passion for creative cooking and his knowledge of diverse local sealife. The result is heavenly cuisine that has captured the attention of critics across the country.

The striking and contemporary, open-kitchen floor plan allows diners to witness the lightening fast and surgeon-like precision of the kitchen staff while poring over a menu that features enticing creations like Crispy Skin Snapper with Sweet & Sour Chard and Tomato Brown Butter or the Roasted Grouper & Braised Collards with Pecan-Shallot Cracklins and Potlikker Jus. This is innovative cooking at its best - fresh, exciting and oh-so-delicious. Voted 'Best Seafood Restaurant' in the country by Bon Apetit.

This is a mecca for dessert lovers- glass cases filled with a vast selection of unique and scrumptious specialty cakes, cheesecakes, cookies, cupcakes and pies, each of them more enticing than the last. Dessert Gallery Bakery & Café is the brainchild of chef and owner Sara Brook who has enjoyed a love affair with sweets and chocolate since childhood.

While working as a paralegal studying to take the LSAT, she discovered that everyone in her law firm was just too serious and the path seemed much too dreary. She decided to instead pursue her passion for baking. 25 years later, Sara still loves poring over recipe books and creating new and interesting combinations and flavors. Brook runs two Houston Dessert Gallery Bakery & Café locations. She ships her desserts nationwide.

DESSERT GALLERY
CARROT CAKE

Even carrot cake 'haters' love this cake! Dessert Gallery's Carrot Cake is an old-fashioned, homemade comfort dessert that's filled with freshly grated carrots, lots of cinnamon, chunks of pineapple and plenty of pecans. It's so moist and yummy, it really takes you back to another time... and the cream cheese frosting is divine!

YIELD: 9-INCH CAKE

CAKE

2 cups	flour		1 teaspoon	salt
2 teaspoons	baking powder		1½ cups	vegetable oil
1½ teaspoons	baking soda		8 ounces	crushed pineapple, with juice
2 teaspoons	cinnamon, generous		2 cups	shredded carrots, generous
1 teaspoon	salt		⅓ cup	pecans
4	eggs			
2 cups	granulated sugar			

Preheat oven to 350 degrees F.

Spray three 9-inch pans with nonstick baking spray.

In a medium bowl or on a flexible prep board, sift together flour, baking powder, baking soda, cinnamon, salt and sugar. Set aside.

In a large bowl, with a hand or stand mixer, beat the eggs, sugar and oil until well mixed.

Add the dry ingredients in small batches and mix on low. Add the pineapple, carrots and nuts and continue to mix on low. Divide batter between the three pans.

Bake for 35 minutes or until a toothpick inserted in the middle comes out clean.

FROSTING

8 ounces	cream cheese, softened (one package)		1 teaspoon	vanilla extract
4 tablespoons	unsalted butter, softened		2 cups	pecan pieces, chopped
4 cups	powdered sugar, sifted			

In a medium bowl, beat the cream cheese until smooth. Add the butter and continue to beat until well mixed and fluffy.

Slowly add the powdered sugar and vanilla and mix until fluffy and smooth.

Ice top and sides of cake with cream cheese frosting.

Press crushed pecans along sides of cake.

In a city where Tex-Mex restaurants are plentiful, El Tiempo Cantina is considered a standout. Owned by the grandsons of Ninfa Laurenzo (of Ninfa's fame) this restaurant is backed with over 55 years of cooking experience and they never disappoint. The outstanding food is fresh, homemade and bursting with flavor. The Spanish-style interior, with antique family photos covering the heavily plastered walls, is an inviting space for casual dinners and fun-filled happy hours.

Every meal begins with their awesome chips and spicy red salsa served alongside the legendary creamy tomatillo salsa - inherited from Mama Ninfa herself. Menu favorites here run the gamut from build-your-own guacamole and crab meat quesadillas to incredible fajitas and a mixed grill that includes fajitas, shrimp, quail, ribs, carnitas, jalapeno sausage and lobster, all served on an anafre (portable grill). Voted Best Chain Restaurant in 2009, this is the cream-of-the-crop for true Tex-Mex lovers.

EL TIEMPO
TRES LECHES CAKE

A spin on the traditional Tres Leches Cake, this recipe calls for adding sour cream to the soaking mixture - technically making it a Quatro Leches Cake. At El Tiempo they layer the cake with fresh fruit and Italian meringue and top it off this way too!

YIELD: 12 SERVINGS

CAKE

1	white cake mix	½ cup	olive oil
3	eggs	1⅔ cups	water

MILK MIXTURE

3 cups	heavy cream	½ cup	sour cream, room temperature
½ cup	buttermilk		
¾ cup plus 2 tablespoons	sweetened condensed milk (7 ounces)		

Preheat oven to 350˚F.

Flour or spray a 9- by-13-inch pan.

In a medium mixing bowl, combine the cake mix and eggs, blending well. Add water and mix well. Next add the olive oil, continuing to mix well.

Pour mixture into the pan and bake for 30 minutes or until toothpick inserted in the middle comes out clean. Let cool.

Remove cake from pan. If any areas of the cake have browned - check the top, bottom and sides- cut them away. You can also trim and discard about half an inch around the edge. Place cake back into pan and poke approximately 18 holes in the top of the cake with a toothpick.

In a large mixing bowl, combine the heavy cream, buttermilk, sweetened condensed milk and mix well. Add the sour cream and blend until smooth.

Pour the milk mixture over the cake to saturate.

Soak the cake well and leave it sitting in the milk mixture so that it penetrates the entire cake. You must be patient and ladle the milk over the top of the cake several times.

Reserve the remaining milk mixture so that you can continue to pour over the cake for 2 or more days if necessary. You want to keep the cake moist.

It is best served in a bowl so that you can pour additional milk over cake as needed.

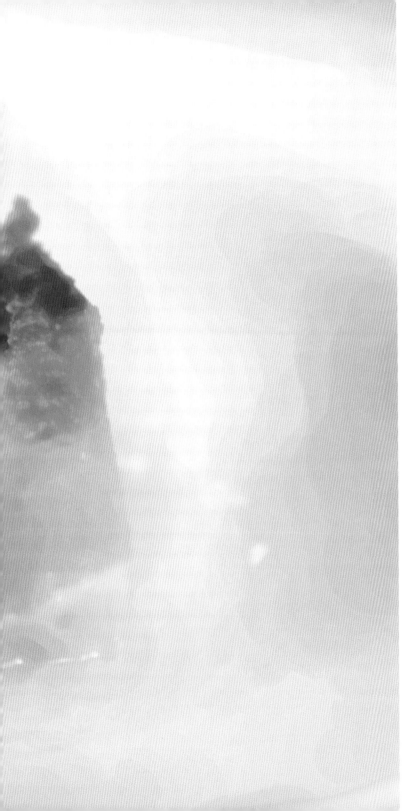

CUSTARDS & PUDDINGS

Egg-thickened custards have been a staple of English cuisine since the 14th century. Like many dessert items, its humble beginnings leaned largely towards the savory. Early recipes suggest ingredients like meat, fish and vegetables, which may sound odd until you realize that a quiche is really nothing more than a savory custard. Eventually, sweeteners and fruits became equally desirable custard ingredients.

Puddings are considered the 'homogenized' cousin of custard. Starches act as the thickening agent instead of eggs, as evidenced by time-honored favorites like rice and bread puddings. Fancier cooks may refer to it as a blancmange - sweetened milk thickened with cornstarch and then cooked.

To be honest, the terms 'pudding' and 'custard' are virtually interchangeable in today's kitchen. It largely falls to the cook preparing the item to make the distinction. If you're hoping to make an impression on the boss at your next dinner party, call it custard... if you're trying to comfort a crying 10-year-old, offer it as pudding.

When making puddings and custards, consider these tips:

-The fresher the cream, the higher the pH level - making it less likely to curdle in the cooking process.

-When refrigerating a just cooked or baked custard, let it cool about 5 to 10 minutes and then cover it with plastic wrap. Make sure it touches the surface of the custard to prevent the milk proteins from forming a thin 'skin' on top when refrigerated.

-Tempering your eggs is a must. If egg yolks are added to a hot liquid all at once, they will scramble. And while scrambled eggs are great for breakfast, they do not, as a rule, make for a good custard.

-A good judge of doneness for a baked custard - the liquid area in the pie's center should be the size of a quarter.

Cross the border into... Louisiana!

Brennan's Houston first opened in 1967 as the sister restaurant to the world-famous Commander's Palace in New Orleans.

Exceptional meals a la Texas creole and lasting memories were served to generations of Houstonians until the restaurant was destroyed by a fire during Hurricane Ike in 2009.

Luckily, eighty percent of the historic building, designed by the great Houston architect, John Staub, was able to be restored.

In true New Orleans style, the restaurant reopened on Fat Tuesday in 2010.

NOTE: When reheating sauce, be sure to use a moderate temperature so the egg in the sauce doesn't curdle.

BRENNAN'S
CREOLE BREAD PUDDING

Who knew soggy bread could taste so irresistible? This is an excellent way to use day old French bread. And not just for the sweet. Savory bread puddings can be easily prepared with a few modifications - a great use for leftover meats and vegetables. It is easy to prepare and can even be assembled a day ahead of time. The saturated ingredients going into the oven will have you proudly beaming when you remove the puffy dish from the oven. The Rye Whiskey Sauce here is delightfully intoxicating. I used true rye whiskey but I think you could use a common blend probably already sitting in your liquor cabinet.

YIELD: 8 TO 12 SERVINGS

3 cups	packed brown sugar		2 cups	whipping cream
2 teaspoons	cinnamon		5 teaspoons	vanilla extract
½ teaspoon	nutmeg		14	bread slices, 1-inch thick
5	eggs, lightly beaten		1 cup	raisins
4 cups	milk		1½ cups	pecan pieces

Preheat the oven to 300°F.

In a large bowl, blend the sugar, cinnamon and nutmeg. Whisk in the eggs, milk, cream and vanilla.

Tear the bread slices into big, bite-sized pieces and place in a lightly buttered 9-by-13-inch pan.

Pour the custard mixture over the bread and allow to soak until soft, about 1 hour. Stir the raisins into the pudding and top with nuts. Bake uncovered 1½ hours.

Prepare the Rye Whiskey Sauce and keep warm until needed.

Scoop the bread pudding into individual bowls and top with the reserved Rye Whiskey Sauce.

RYE WHISKEY SAUCE

2 cups	whipping cream		2 tablespoons	cold water
9 tablespoons	granulated sugar		2	egg yolks
1½ tablespoons	cornstarch		¼ cup	rye whiskey

Heat the cream and sugar in a heavy-bottomed medium saucepan over medium-high heat until mixture begins to boil.

Mix the cornstarch and cold water in a small bowl until smooth; slowly whisk into simmering cream. Simmer 2 to 3 minutes.

Put the yolks into a stainless steel bowl; whisk. Temper the yolks by slowly whisking 1 cup hot, thickened cream mixture into yolks. Return the yolk mixture to hot cream mixture, whisking in slowly. After the mixture is whisked together, cook over medium-low heat until mixture reaches 140°F. Remove from heat and pour through a fine mesh strainer.

Add the whiskey, adjusting to taste, and keep warm until ready to use.

Store sauce in a covered container in the refrigerator up to 3 days.

LEXINGTON GRILLE
CRÈME BRÛLÉE

A classic finale to any meal, Lexington Grille's Crème Brûlée combines tastes and textures that are simultaneously light and sinful. The divinely creamy, vanilla-infused custard is sealed in a crunchy, sugary shell that shatters like glass when hit with the back of your spoon.

You can use the broiler to caramelize the top but a small blowtorch will yield better results and is much more thrilling to watch!

YIELD: SIX 8-OUNCE SERVINGS

4 cups	heavy cream		6	egg yolks
6 tablespoons	granulated sugar		1½ tablespoons	Grand Marnier
2	vanilla beans, halved lengthwise, seeds scraped		4 tablespoons	brown sugar
			6 cups	hot water

Preheat oven to 350°F.

Place the ramekins in a roasting pan lined with a dishcloth.

In a saucepan over medium heat, combine the cream, sugar and vanilla bean seeds. Stir constantly until sugar dissolves and the mixture begins to boil slightly. Remove from heat. Pour the mixture into a glass bowl and place in freezer for 10 minutes.

In a large bowl, mix the egg yolks and the Grand Marnier until well combined.

Combine the cooled cream mixture and the eggs.

Divide the custard between the ramekins and place in oven. Pour the hot water into the roasting pan until it reaches halfway up the sides of the ramekins, being careful not to splash water in the custard.

Bake for 45 to 50 minutes or until the crème brûlée is set. It will still jiggle quite a bit.

Remove the ramekins from the pan. Cool to room temperature and refrigerate until chilled, at least 2 hours. It is best to refrigerate overnight.

Sprinkle a layer of brown sugar over the top of each cup. Place the cups on a sheet pan and set under a hot broiler until the sugar melts, darkens and forms a crust. This is the brûlée process, so watch it carefully. A small butane torch may also be used to caramelize the sugar topping. As the sugar crust cools, it hardens.

My husband Billy and I had our first date at the Lexington Grille, so it definitely holds a special place in my heart. A cozy, restored house hidden in the Upper Kirby District of Houston creates the perfect, intimate setting complete with dark, rich woodwork and plenty of romantic ambiance. It is beautiful and sophisticated, much like the food they create.

Attention to detail is the specialty here. In a city where trendy restaurants are done, redone and overdone - things are always perfect at this 15 year veteran establishment. From the pesto dipping sauce for the bread to the crab cakes and stuffed shrimp, you really can't go wrong. My husband's absolute favorite - the Filet Mignon with a Creamy Gorgonzola Port Wine Sauce - is not to be missed and the Lexington Chicken (stuffed with spinach, mushrooms, artichokes and sun-dried tomatoes) served with a Shallot and Marsala Sauce is out of this world. And who knows... you may fall in love there, too.

If you are in search of truly authentic Mexican cuisine in Houston, Hugo's (in the heart of the Montrose neighborhood) is the superlative definition. Co-owner, Executive Chef and namesake Hugo Ortega is the mastermind behind the menu here and it reflects his dedication to authentic, fresh and earthy food that showcases the regional cooking of Mexico.

Ortega, who climbed the ranks from busboy to award-winning chef and owner, pays tribute to his homeland with a menu that represents Mexico's regions through their culinary techniques, flavors and ingredients. From recipes as deep and complex as the moles of Oaxaca to something as earthy and simple as a homemade corn tortilla, Hugo's is all about the culinary roots of a dish. They roast and grind their own chocolate, coffee and corn and they make their own queso fresco, chorizo and tortillas. This is the real deal and critics and diners alike rank it among the best restaurants in America.

HUGO'S
FLAN DE QUESO

I was never a fan of flan, until I had Ruben Ortega's. This luscious, creamy, vanilla flan is a cross between egg custard and cheesecake. Served with passion fruit sauce and strawberries, Ruben tops it with chantilly cream (that's just vanilla flavored whipped cream) and candied pistachios.

Be sure not to overcook - if your flan has bubbles in it, that's *just* what you've done.

YIELD: SIX 8-OUNCE SERVINGS

CARAMEL

¼ cup	water		1 cup	granulated sugar

In a saucepan, bring the water and the sugar to boil, stirring until sugar dissolves. Lower the heat and burn the sugar into a soft caramel. Immediately pour caramel into the ramekins, tipping quickly to coat the bottoms. Set aside to let cool.

FLAN

6 ounces	cream cheese, softened		1 tablespoon	vanilla
3	eggs		1 can plus	sweetened condensed
3	egg yolks		7 tablespoons	milk (17.5 ounces)
2 cups	milk		¾ cup	water

Preheat oven to 325˚F.

In a large bowl, using a hand mixer, beat the cream cheese until soft. Beat in eggs, one at time, until well combined. Continuing to beat, add the milk, one half cup at a time. Then add the vanilla and sweetened condensed milk, mixing well. Sieve the mix. Set aside.

Put the caramel coated ramekins on top of a dish towel inside a 3-inch deep baking pan. Fill each of the caramel coated ramekins with the liquid custard.

Fill the larger pan three-quarters full of hot water. Cook for about 40 to 50 minutes, until the center of the flan is pretty firm.

Allow to cool and serve at room temperature or chilled. Loosen the edges with a knife before inverting on a plate to serve.

NOTE: A dish cloth, rings or cookie cutters placed in between the 2 pans will help with even heat distribution and avoid scorching.

TONY'S
APRICOT SOUFFLE

Tony's serves over 30 different types of souffles and the same gentleman has been making them for the past 14 years. Long time customers never miss the opportunity to order one. The Apricot Souffle is an elegant dessert with tangy apricot flavors enhanced with a warm apricot caramel. It's the perfect balance of flavors with the tart sweetness of the apricots and the richness of the caramel.

YIELD: 8-CUP SOUFFLE

2 cups	dried apricots		8	eggs, separated
2½ cups	boiling water		11 ounces	cream cheese, softened
1¼ cups	sugar			
2 cups	milk		1 tablespoon	Kirsch
3 tablespoons	unsalted butter		for dusting	powdered sugar
6 tablespoons	all-purpose flour			

Put the apricots in a small pot. Pour the boiling water over, cover, and put aside for 1 hour.

Next, stir in the sugar, bring to a simmer and cook uncovered for 20 minutes. Cool for 20 minutes.

Strain three quarters of the liquid and discard. Transfer mixture to a blender or food processor and puree. Set aside 1½ cups of the puree for the souffle. The remaining puree will be used in the sauce.

Preheat the oven to 350˚F.

In a 2-quart saucepan, heat the milk on medium heat. In a separate saucepan, melt the butter and stir in the flour. Stir and cook for two minutes. Add the warmed milk, and stir constantly over medium-low heat until smooth and thick. This takes 3 to 5 minutes.

In a large bowl, beat egg yolks with a fork or whisk. Pour a small amount of milk sauce in the egg yolks. Beat together, then add the remaining milk sauce in thirds. Whisk in the apricot puree, cream cheese and Kirsch, blending well. Beat the egg white to medium peaks. Fold half of the beaten egg whites into the egg yolk mixture. Gently fold in the remaining egg whites.

Pour mixture in a well-greased soufflé dish. If desired, put a rim of parchment or aluminum foil around the top of the dish as a collar (this must also be greased). Bake for 40 to 45 minutes. Test with knife.

Sprinkle powdered sugar over and serve at once.

NOTE: This should produce a soufflé that is still soft in the center. The slightly 'custardy' center serves as a sauce to spoon over the rest of the soufflé. If you want, you can bake the soufflé longer and make the apricot caramel sauce to serve with it.

This world-class restaurant has been around for over 45 years. The European style, Italian infused menu is always stellar.

Tony Vallone's motto is "First in season, first at Tony's".

APRICOT CARAMEL SAUCE

2 cups	granulated sugar
¾ cup	unsalted butter
1 cup	heavy whipping cream
½ cup	pureed apricots (same as in soufflé)
⅓ cup	apricot nectar

Heat the sugar on moderately high heat in a heavy bottomed 2-quart or 3-quart saucepan. As the sugar begins to melt, stir vigorously with a whisk or wooden spoon. As soon as the sugar comes to a boil, stop stirring.

As soon as all of the sugar crystals have melted immediately add the butter to the pan. Whisk until the butter has melted.

Once the butter has melted, take the pan off the heat. Slowly add the heavy whipping cream to the pan and continue to whisk to incorporate. The mixture will foam up.

Whisk until the caramel sauce is smooth. Add the pureed apricots and apricot nectar. Let cool in the pan for a couple of minutes.

Critically acclaimed Feast has only been around since 2008, but they jumped directly into the spotlight. The rustic European-style restaurant is owned and operated by Richard Knight and James and Meagan Silk who created a warm and comfortable concept restaurant around the locavore movement - using only foods grown or produced locally. The menu here, which changes daily, also features the names and locations of the farms, growers and ranches from which every menu item was procured.

British chefs Richard Knight and James Silk are disciples of Fergus Henderson, a chef known for his offal cookery and a cookbook called 'The Whole Beast.' The food here is hearty and satisfying. The menu also includes several dishes for 'innards-lovers' (traditional fare for these British-born chefs) but, there's plenty of seafood among the entrees along with lamb shanks, chicken and usually at least one vegetarian creation. Knight suggests you be adventurous. That is, after all, part of the pleasure of eating.

FEAST
STICKY TOFFEE PUDDING

This very traditional British dessert has become all the rage here in the U.S. - perhaps due in part to 'O' magazine referring to the sensual treat as the, "sexiest English creation since Colin Firth." This warm, date-filled cake is drenched in toffee sauce and served with a dollop of clotted cream (reduced, unsweetened, savory cream.)

YIELD: SIX 8-OUNCE SERVINGS

PUDDING

1 cup	dates, pitted, chopped		1/3 cup	superfine sugar
1 teaspoon	baking soda		2	eggs
1⅛ cups	hot water		1 cup	self-rising flour
6 tablespoons	unsalted butter, softened			

Preheat the oven to 350°F.

In a bowl, mix the dates, baking soda and the water together and leave to soak for ten minutes.

In a clean bowl, cream the butter and sugar together until light and fluffy.

Still stirring the butter mixture, gradually add the eggs, making sure they are well combined.

Still stirring, gradually add the flour, then add the date mixture.

Pour the mixture into ramekins and place into the oven and bake for 35 to 40 minutes, or until cooked through.

TOFFEE SAUCE

¾ cup plus 2 tablespoons	unsalted butter (7 ounces)		1¾ cups	brown sugar
			1	vanilla pod, split
			1⅛ cups	heavy cream

In a heavy-bottomed pan over medium heat, melt the butter.

Add the brown sugar, vanilla pod and cream and stir well. Simmer for 5 minutes.

To serve, spoon out a portion of the pudding onto a plate and pour the hot toffee sauce over.

The toffee sauce is also lovely over ice cream.

*17 / ALDEN HOTEL

DECONSTRUCTED BANANAS FOSTER

At *17 they make everything from scratch, including the graham crackers and the ice cream for this dessert. This deconstructed classic will still be surprisingly good if you want to save time by buying a box of cinnamon-topped graham crackers and a high-end caramel gelato or ice cream. However, if you go that route, do NOT use fat free or low-calorie products. As Executive Sous Chef Sam Beier says, "*Guilt is one of the flavors that makes this dish so good.*"

YIELD: 6 SERVINGS

BROWN BUTTER ICE CREAM

8 tablespoons	unsalted butter		2½ cups	heavy cream
⅓ cup	brown sugar		½ cup	2% milk
⅓ cup	granulated sugar		1 tablespoon	vanilla extract
6	egg yolks		pinch	salt, large
1 tablespoon	vanilla extract			

Place butter into a pan and cook until brown. Strain and cool.

In a large bowl, mix the sugars, salt, yolks and vanilla and beat at medium speed with an electric mixer until pale in color.

In a medium-sized pot, combine the milk and cream. Place over medium high heat until boiling, stirring occasionally. Slowly incorporate the hot milk into the yolk mixture, return to pot and bring to a boil. Add in the brown butter.

Let mixture cool to room temperature, then place in refrigerator and chill. Follow procedures provided with your ice cream maker to finish making ice cream. Store in freezer.

BANANAS

6	ripe but firm bananas		1 cup	granulated sugar

Cut bananas crossways into scallop shapes about 1½-inches wide. Dip one end of the banana in sugar and, using a torch, quickly brulee the sugar. Set aside.

BOURBON SAUCE

1 cup	heavy cream		½ cup	bourbon
6	egg yolks		2 tablespoons	banana liqueur
¼ cup	sugar			

In a large bowl using an electric mixer, whip cream until it ribbons (should not hold a peak).

In a double boiler, whisk yolks and sugar until slightly thickened, about 5 minutes. Add the bourbon and the liqueur and cook for 2 more minutes. Fold in whipped cream.

Arrange bananas on one side of the plates, add a scoop of ice cream on the other. Place a graham cracker in between and serve with a side of bourbon sauce.

*The historic Sam Houston hotel opened almost a century ago, but step inside now and tradition has been transformed into a sleek and high-tech, luxury, boutique hotel. Classic architecture and cutting-edge, contemporary design have turned the Sam Houston into the newly-named Alden Houston in the heart of downtown. The award-winning, in-house restaurant - *17 - garners as much attention as the hotel itself.*

*Illuminated by sparkling rectangular chandeliers and walls adorned with red silk, *17 is the familiar with a modern twist. Winner of Best Interior Design, the space is a stunning reminder of just how fine dining can be. The cuisine is New American with clean, bold flavors and they offer a conveniently timed pre-theatre menu for fans of the footlights.*

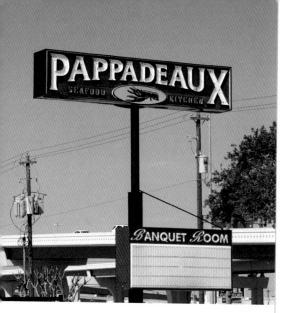

The fun and festivity of the French Quarter has been alive at Pappadeaux Seafood Kitchen since 1986.

Pappadeaux (pronounced pa-puh-doe) serves up the freshest seafood and Louisiana-style favorites like Blackened Opelousas Fillet, Crawfish & Shrimp Fondeaux, and Seafood Gumbo. The menu offers a great selection including a wide variety of fresh, flavorful fish, giant salads, rich and delicious appetizers. These are complemented by a carefully designed specialty drink menu and finished off with homemade, delectable desserts so huge you'll be able to share them with the family. Pappadeaux delivers the spirit of Mardis Gras all year long.

WHIPPED CREAM

½ cup	heavy cream
2 tablespoons	granulated sugar

Whisk heavy cream and granulated sugar in a mixing bowl until the cream holds stiff peaks. Store in refrigerator until needed.

PAPPADEAUX
BANANA PUDDING

When the Banana Pudding was added to the dessert menu at Pappadeaux, it was only meant to be served during the summer. But when the first summer came to a close and it was pulled from the dessert menu, guests became unruly- they just couldn't get enough! When they asked their guests what they loved so much about the dish, they were regaled with stories of their youth and the utter delight and anticipation they felt when their mothers and grandmothers pulled the cool mason jar out of the refrigerator filled to the top with cold pastry cream, sliced bananas, and crunchy vanilla wafers.

The Pappas Family could not deny their guests such joy! Banana Pudding was quickly brought back by popular demand and has been a mainstay on the menu ever since.

YIELD: 2 SERVINGS

26	vanilla wafers		1½ cups	pastry cream
24	banana slices, ½-inch thick		4 tablespoons	whipped cream
			2	strawberries

Break 6 vanilla wafers into the bottom of each mason jar.

Place 6 banana slices on top of the broken cookies in each jar.

Spoon 6 tablespoons of pastry cream into each jar; lightly tap the jar on the table to remove any air bubbles. Repeat layers once more, starting with broken wafers, banana slices, then pastry cream.

Finish the jars by layering with a dollop of whip cream on the top.

Place vanilla wafer into whipped cream and place strawberry on the lip of the jar.

Dust entire dish with powdered sugar.

PASTRY CREAM

2½ cups	whole milk		2 tablespoons	cornstarch
3	eggs, extra large		1 teaspoons	vanilla extract
½ cup plus 2 tablespoons	granulated sugar		½ tablespoon	unsalted butter

In a sauce pan, heat the milk to just below boiling.

Place the sugar, eggs, and cornstarch in a large mixing bowl and whisk to combine.

Slowly pour a portion of the warm milk into the sugar and egg mixture, stirring constantly.

Once incorporated, pour mixture back into the sauce pot with the remaining milk.

Place over medium low heat and stir constantly to thicken cream and avoid any sticking. Cook until the mixture is thick and leaves a trail when the whisk is pulled through the cream.

Strain cream through a fine mesh sieve into a mixing bowl. Whisk in vanilla extract and unsalted butter until completely incorporated, or blend with an immersion blender for 30 seconds. Place a piece of plastic wrap directly on top of the cream (this will prevent a skin from forming) and chill in refrigerator.

RUGGLES GRILL
WHITE CHOCOLATE BREAD PUDDING

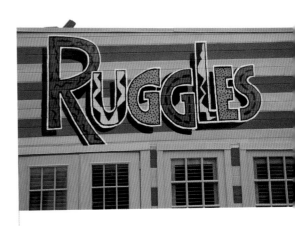

Here's a familiar flavor - pushed over the edge. And, you get a two-for-one here: bread pudding and créme brûlée in one! This velvety dessert melts in your mouth. The toasty crunch of the bread pudding crust followed by a smooth, creamy custard. It's no surprise that it has been the star of the dessert tray at Ruggles Grill for over two decades.

YIELD: 12 SERVINGS

2 cups	heavy whipping cream
2 cups	half-and-half
8 ounces	white baking bars, cut into ¼- to ½-inch pieces
1½ cups	granulated sugar
8	egg yolks
1 teaspoon	vanilla
¼ teaspoon	salt
1	baguette, about 25 ½-inch slices
1 package	frozen raspberries, thawed, (12 ounces)
for garnish	sliced almonds

Heat oven to 325˚F.

Grease a 9-by-13-inch casserole.

In a 3-quart saucepan, heat whipping cream and half and half to boiling over medium heat, stirring constantly. Stir in baking bar pieces and remove from heat. Beat the sugar, egg yolks, vanilla, and salt until creamy. Gradually add cream mixture, beating constantly until smooth.

Line casserole with baguette slices. Pour 2 cups of the cream mixture over bread. Let stand a few minutes until bread absorbs mixture. Add remaining baguette slices. Pour remaining mixture over bread, 2 cups at a time; let stand a few minutes until bread absorbs mixture. Sprinkle with almonds and decorating sugar, if desired.

Place casserole in roasting pan and place in the oven. Pour boiling water into roasting pan until 1-inch deep.

Bake uncovered for 45 minutes. Remove from oven, cover with foil (shiny side down) and continue to bake for 1 hour or until a knife inserted 1-inch from edge comes out clean.

Blend the raspberries until smooth and strain seeds. Serve with the raspberry sauce and if desired, fresh raspberries.

Ruggles Grill has been an esteemed Houston restaurant for over 35 years. When they suffered substantial damages during Hurricane Ike, they took the opportunity to revamp the menu and pioneer the 'green' philosophy of cooking, becoming Certified by the Green Restaurant Association when they reopened in 2010. Since then, Executive Chef and Owner Bruce Molzan and company have taken 'farm-to-table' to the next level.

The delicious menu offers items that incorporate organic, all-natural, hormone-free, preservative-free products with fine dining flair. Mix that with the festive environment and great ambiance and music that made Ruggles a star in the 80's and 90's, and you have an all new experience that is fast becoming a star all over again.

The latest delicious escapade by acclaimed restaurateurs Arturo Boada and Bill Sadler is Arturo's Uptown Italiano, yet another superb establishment from the team behind Beso & Solero - two of my favorite Houston hangouts.

Chef Arturo is famous for his Latino flair, but he's also half Italian and grew up savoring Mama Sonia Merendoni's cooking in the family kitchen. Her influence inspires Chef Arturo and her beloved Italian landscapes are splashed across the restaurant walls.

Classic high notes include savory raviolis and rich Eggplant Parmigiana. Flourishes from the dessert menu include silky Panna Cotta, creamy Tiramisu and irresistible Crema Catalana, each a celebration of sweet memories.

ARTURO'S UPTOWN ITALIANO
Crèma Catalana

Crèma Catalana is silky smooth custard with a hint of vanilla, topped with caramelized brown sugar for the perfect balance of crunch and cream in every heavenly bite. It is served on individual spoons so everyone at the table may share it.

YIELD: 20 TO 30 SPOONFULS

2½ cups	heavy whipping cream	½ teaspoon	vanilla extract
6 large	egg yolks	½ cup	brown sugar
½ cup	granulated sugar		

Preheat oven to 350°F.

In a large saucepan over medium low heat, heat the cream to 140°F. Remove the cream from the heat and set aside.

In a separate large stainless mixing bowl, combine the egg yolks, sugar and vanilla and mix well with a whisk. Slowly add the cream and continue to whisk until well blended.

Pour into a 8-by-8-inch pan and cover tightly with aluminum foil (shiny side down). Carefully set the pan inside of a larger pan partially filled with lukewarm water, about ½-inch below the top of the smaller pan when the two are placed together. Carefully place in the oven and bake in the water bath for 45 to 60 minutes. Gently remove the custard pan from the water bath and cool to room temperature. Cover and refrigerate for at least 1 hour.

Scoop the custard into soup or serving spoons. Sprinkle a teaspoon of brown sugar on top of each spoon. Caramelize the sugar with a cook's butane torch and serve immediately.

NOTE: Inexpensive butane cooking torches are available at most specialty stores. When using one be very careful to avoid draperies and other flammable objects. If a torch is not available, make do by placing an oven rack in the highest position, putting the oven on broil, cover a sheet pan with aluminum foil and crimp the foil around each spoon to rest it securely. Place in oven under broiler. Watch carefully since the brown sugar will bubble then quickly burn.

PIES & TARTS

Pie is not what it used to be. But that's a good thing. From it's first recorded use by Egyptians in 6500 B.C. and until the mid 1500's, the pastry shell was used solely as a vessel for cooking, serving and storing and was not intended to be eaten. Often several inches thick to withstand hours of baking, the crust on those early pies was the only baking container used by cooks, thereby making virtually everything... a pie.

Thankfully, folks eventually figured out that pie crust could be flaky and delicious. But, pies remained a savory foodstuff until the 1600's when Native Americans directed the first American settlers to try berries and fruits. Before long, the apple would make its way into the ingredient list and the standard by which all things 'American' are judged would become one of our nation's first culinary contributions to the world.

A tart, usually fruit or custard filled, is similar enough to a pie - the distinction that sets it apart is largely the container in which it is prepared. Tarts pans are traditionally more straight-sided than pie pans and generally feature a removable ring that allows the tart to be completely removed from the baking vessel for serving.

When making pies or tarts, consider these useful tips while baking:

-A teaspoon of vinegar or lemon juice as part of your liquid for each cup of flour in pastry and pie dough recipes won't affect the flavor but will result in more tender baked products.

-You can keep meringue from 'weeping' or 'sweating after baking by spreading it over the pie while the filling is still warm.

-Prevent soggy blind-baked crust by brushing the shell with melted butter and refrigerating for a bit before filling.

This contemporary eatery is located in a renovated commercial building in the heart of the Heights' 19th Street business district. Simple table settings set the stage for creative, value-driven, seasonal and inventive menus. 'Global Home Cooking' is taken to the next level here.

WHIPPED CREAM

1 cup	heavy whipping cream
1½ tablespoons	powdered sugar

Whip the cream to soft peaks.

To assemble, put a dollop of the chilled coconut cream filling in each toasted and cooled shell. Top with some whipped cream and sprinkle with the remaining toasted coconut.

NOTE: They use 3-inch non-stick fluted pans at Shade (which you can purchase at Sur la Table).

SHADE
COCONUT CREAM TART

This tried and true classic American dessert is always the top seller at Shade. It has been on the menu since they opened and continues to please the dessert dining patrons year after year. The individual tart shells add a sophisticated touch to a rewarding comfort food dessert experience. All of the components may be made ahead of time and then quickly assembled for dessert at just the right time.

YIELD: EIGHT 3-INCH TARTS OR TWO 8-INCH TARTS

CRUST

¾ cup plus 2 tablespoons	unsalted butter, (7 ounces)		¼ teaspoon	vanilla
¾ cup	granulated sugar		pinch	baking soda
½	egg, whisked		1¼ cups	bread flour
			¼ pound	hazelnuts, toasted crushed & cooled

Preheat oven to 325°F (convection oven) or 350°F (regular oven).

In a mixing bowl, using a stand or hand mixer, cream the butter and sugar. Add the egg and vanilla.

Fold in the bread flour, pinch of soda and toasted hazelnuts.

Refrigerate the dough for 4 hours before using. It will need to be firm to handle.

Roll the dough between pieces of plastic wrap and press into either small individual tart shells or two 8-inch tart shells, making sure to build the crust up the sides of the shells. Freeze the shells before par baking. Blind bake the shells until light golden brown, about 14 to 18 minutes for convection and 20 to 25 minutes in regular oven.

TOASTED COCONUT

2½ cups	coconut, sweetened & shredded

Spread the coconut on a sheet pan and bake at 350°F until light brown, about 10 to 15 minutes.

FILLING

¾ cup	all-purpose flour		4	egg yolks
1 cup	granulated sugar		2 tablespoons	butter
½ teaspoon	salt		½ tablespoon	vanilla
2⅓ cups	2% milk		2 cups	toasted coconut, cooled
1 cup	heavy cream			

Sift the flour and sugar into a bowl that will be placed over a water bath. Gradually whisk in the milk and cook over a double boiler, constantly stirring, making sure to keep the mixture off the sides for about 20 minutes, or until thick. Whisk egg yolks in another bowl, slowly temper a bit of the milk mixture into egg yolks and put back over the heat and cook for 2 minutes more. Remove the mixture from heat and add butter and vanilla. Cool completely. Once the mixture is completely cooled, fold in 2 cups of the toasted and cooled coconut.

THE RAINBOW LODGE
BAKLAVA TART

Many historians say that baklava is the original dessert. The recipe for this modern classic is a collaboration between Chef & Pastry Chef, Mark Schmidt and Julie Ann Nielsen. Here, the honey and walnuts of Greek baklava and the almonds of the French frangipani have been replaced with pistachios and orange filling and served with honey ice cream and black olive caramel - yes, you read that right - black olive caramel! The black olive caramel is delicious and equally as wonderful with shellfish and foie gras.

YIELD: 8 TARTS

FILLING

6 ounces	pistachios, finely ground (raw)		6 tablespoons	unsalted butter, room temperature
¾ cup	granulated sugar		2	eggs
½ tablespoon	orange zest		½ teaspoon	cinnamon
¼ teaspoon	baking powder		¼ teaspoon	clove
			¼ teaspoon	nutmeg

Combine all ingredients in a food processor until fully blended. Set aside.

SHELLS

1 package	phyllo dough, thawed completely at room temperature		1 cup	unsalted butter, melted (8 ounces)

Preheat oven to 350°F.

Lay one sheet of the phyllo flat on counter, brush with melted butter. Repeat 2 more times. Slice each sheet into 6 equal squares. This will make 2 tarts. Fan three squares on top of each other and mold into a muffin tin. Repeat this whole process three more times.

Fill the phyllo shells with the filling and sprinkle some ground pistachios on top. Bake for 16 minutes or until the filling is lightly and evenly browned.

HONEY ICE CREAM

4	egg yolks		⅛ teaspoon	salt
⅔ cup	honey		3 cups	heavy cream

In a small bowl, whisk together the eggs, honey and salt. Set aside.

In a medium saucepan, bring the heavy cream to a simmer. While constantly whisking, slowly pour the milk into the egg mixture.

Return to the saucepan and continually stir over medium to low heat until the mixture just thickens. Immediately remove from the heat and strain.

Let cool and then refrigerate before spinning in an ice cream machine.

Serve the tart topped with ice cream and drizzled with the caramel and syrup.

BLACK OLIVE CARAMEL

1½ cups	granulated sugar
½ cup	water
¾ cup	heavy cream
⅓ cup	black olives, blended to a paste

In a saucepan, over medium heat, bring the sugar and water to a boil. Continue cooking the sugar until it reaches a medium amber color. Very slowly pour the heavy cream into the sugar, it will bubble and steam, be careful! Whisk until all the sugar is melted, remove from the heat and add the olive paste. Strain into a heat-proof container and refrigerate until thick.

SYRUP

¾ cup	granulated sugar
½ cup	water
1	orange rind

Combine the sugar, water and rind in a saucepan. Bring to a boil and continue boiling for 5 minutes. Strain into a heat-proof container and refrigerate.

High style, culinary excellence and ambience have been drawing folks to Ibiza for almost 10 years now. A collaboration of Chef Charles Clark and Grant Cooper, this wonderfully unpretentious restaurant has received accolades from Food & Wine, Bon Appétit and Wine Spectator magazines.

Chef Charles Clark forms a smartly composed mix of Spanish, French and Mediterranean cuisines with farm-fresh, local and seasonal ingredients. Also known for their reasonably priced wine, the dramatic centerpiece of the restaurant is the towering 25-foot wine wall that holds 4,000 bottles.

Chef Clark appeared on an episode of Iron Chef -'Battle Halibut', where he competed against Chef Mario Batali and the olive oil, poached halibut he prepared on the show is now a hot menu item here.

IBIZA
LEMON MERINGUE TART

Lemon meringue recipes get passed down from generation to generation. This one is a tribute to Rebecca Masson's great grandmother. This was one of the first desserts put on the menu at Ibiza and it has stood the test of time. In the winter, you can use Meyer lemons for a different lemon flavor. Just make sure to always use fresh lemon juice. Pucker up!

YIELD: 9-INCH TART

CRUST

| 6 tablespoons | unsalted butter, melted | ¼ cup | granulated sugar |
| 1½ cups | graham cracker crumbs | pinch | salt |

Preheat oven to 350°F.

Combine all the ingredients in a bowl and mix together. Press into a 9-inch tart mold firmly and up the edges. Bake for 8 to 10 minutes.

Let cool.

FILLING

3	large eggs	3 tablespoons	unsalted butter
½ cup plus		3	lemons, juiced
1 tablespoon	granulated sugar		

Fill a medium saucepan with water and bring to a simmer.

Put lemon juice and eggs in a bowl and whisk to combine. Add the sugar and butter and combine. Place bowl over simmering water, the water can not touch the bowl. Whisk constantly, until the butter is melted, mixture is smooth and slightly thickened. Remove from heat and let cool for 15 minutes.

Put tart shell on a baking sheet. Pour filling into shell and bake for 8 to 10 minutes or until the center is just set. Cool completely.

MERINGUE

| 1 cup | superfine sugar | 5 | egg whites, room temperature |
| ¼ cup | water | ¼ teaspoon | cream of tartar |

In a small pot over low heat, combine sugar and water. Swirl the pot over the burner to dissolve the sugar completely. Do not stir. Increase the heat and boil to soft-ball stage (235°-240°F). Use a candy thermometer for accuracy. Wash down the inside wall of the pot with a wet pastry brush. This will help prevent sugar crystals from forming around the sides, falling in and causing a chain reaction.

In the bowl of an electric mixer, whip the eggs whites on low speed until foamy. Add the cream of tartar, increase the speed to medium, and beat until soft peaks form.

With the mixer running, pour the hot sugar syrup in a thin stream over fluffed egg whites. Beat until the egg whites are stiff and glossy. Be sure the tart has completely cooled before spreading the meringue. Using a blow torch is the best way to brown the meringue or you can place the tart under the broiler for a few minutes.

BACKSTREET CAFE
Drunken Cherry Clafoutis

Clafoutis? Never heard of it?

It is of French origin - a cross between a pie, a custard and a pancake. The name comes from an old Occitan word meaning "to fill up."

Made with almond flour, it is light in texture, heartily satisfying and gluten-free. The fresh, drunken, cherries make this dessert come alive in your mouth. If fresh cherries aren't in season, other fruits that are just as heavenly in the clafoutis are berries, apples, pears, peaches or grapes.

YIELD: EIGHT 6-OUNCE SERVINGS

NOTE: Drunken cherries may be found at the supermarket, but if you are buying fresh, this is how to make them.

DRUNKEN CHERRIES

1 cup	granulated sugar	1 ½ cups	Bing cherries (pitted)
½ cup	water	½ cup	brandy

Bring sugar and water to a boil. Add cherries and cook for 3 minutes. Remove from stove and mix in brandy. Rest for 1 day.

CLAFOUTIS

½ cup plus 6 tablespoons	unsalted butter (7 ounces)	5 teaspoons	cornstarch
1¾ cups	powdered sugar	4	eggs
2 cups	almond flour	1 cup	drunken cherries

Preheat oven to 325˚F.

In a medium bowl, using a hand or stand mixer, cream the softened butter and sugar together. Add the almond flour and cornstarch, until fully combined. Slowly add the eggs, one at a time, fully incorporating each. Beat at medium speed until light and fluffy. Set aside.

Coat eight 6-ounce individual ramekins with non-stick spray. Scoop a little less than half a cup of batter into each ramekin and arrange cherries sparingly in batter.

Bake for approximately 15 minutes, until golden brown.

SERVING SUGGESTION: At Backstreet, they serve the Cherry Clafoutis with homemade pistachio ice cream and crushed roasted pistachios. A good, creamy vanilla ice cream will work as well.

Housed in a picturesque 1930's-era home on the fringe of Houston's River Oaks neighborhood is Backstreet Cafe, an iconic and innovative New American Bistro that has been serving diners for more than a quarter-century. Visionary Owner Tracy Vaught transformed the former residence into a comfortably chic eatery that features intimate dining throughout and al fresco dining on the lush, New Orleans-style patio.

Executive Chef Hugo Ortega oversees the creation of the imaginative cuisine. Freshness and originality are key to the award-winning chef, who utilizes diverse ingredients and techniques while maintaining a uniquely American vibe.

Lunchtime favorites here include the Crispy Lobster Sandwich on toasted brioche with red pepper remoulade, and the Charred Tomato Tortilla Soup, one of Houston's best renditions of this regional favorite. And not-to-be-missed from the dinner menu is the hearty Backstreet Meatloaf Tower - beef and veal meatloaf with garlic mashed potatoes, sautéed spinach and wild mushroom gravy.

Mark's is a lauded fixture of the Houston culinary scene. Located in a beautifully renovated former church, the space is a fitting backdrop for the worship of delicious food. Vaulted gold ceilings, hand-painted Art Deco murals and candlelight create an ambiance that lulls you into an intimate dining experience unlike any other. Voted Houston's most romantic restaurant, it a memorable experience in every way.

Chef Mark Cox expertly prepares his own brand of American progressive cuisine at Mark's. The menu here draws inspiration from around the globe, indicative of America's true 'melting pot' heritage. Guests choose from a variety of menus: a seasonal menu that reflects what is fresh and in season, the chef's 'personal choices' menu which is changed twice daily and a unique specials menu that is changed numerous times throughout the day to showcase world-class ingredients that have just arrived or have just finished preparation.

MARK'S
BLUEBERRY TART

This dish was developed shortly after opening and has been served every year since! While no always on the menu, some folks call ahead and request it.

A buttery graham cracker crust filled with a creamy mascarpone, almond and blueberry concoction and topped with blueberry compote and blueberry muffin ice cream, Chef Mark likes to say that it's like having breakfast, lunch and a snack... all in one.

YIELD: SIX 8-OUNCE TARTS

SHELL

2½ cups	graham cracker crumbs		1 teaspoon	cinnamon
¼ cup	granulated sugar		½ cup	unsalted butter, melted (4 ounces)

Preheat oven to 350˚F.

Combine all ingredients in a large bowl. Mix until well incorporated. Line the 4-inch tart pans with the graham cracker mixture (about a handful) and bake until golden brown, approximately 5 to 10 minutes.

FILLING

¾ cup	sliced almonds		1 cup	heavy cream
¾ cup	powdered sugar		1 cup	mascarpone cheese
2	eggs			

Place all ingredients in the bowl of a food processor and process until smooth.

BLUEBERRY COMPOTE

1	lemon		½ cup plus	
2 tablespoons	cornstarch		1 tablespoon	granulated sugar
1 pint	blueberries		1 tablespoon	water

Preheat the oven to 325˚F.

Zest and juice the lemon. Combine with the cornstarch and set aside.

Place the blueberries, sugar and water in a sauce pan and bring to a boil.

Pour the lemon mixture into the pan and continue cooking until thick.

Place a tablespoon of the blueberry mixture on the bottom of each tart shell. (The leftover portion is used to garnish the top of the tart after baking).

Top off the shell with the mascarpone filling.

Bake for 20 to 25 minutes or until tart is set.

Cool to room temperature.

Garnish with the remaining compote and top with a scoop of blueberry ice cream.

CHEZ NOUS
CHOCOLATE CABERNET TART

Chocoholics and wine-lovers rejoice, this one dessert has you covered on both counts. The Cabernet infuses just enough acidity to contrast and heighten the chocolatey richness of this decadent creation. The quality of ingredients used is important here - Chez Nous uses only Belgian Callebut chocolate for this unique tart.

YIELD: 9-INCH PIE

CRUST

1⅔ cups	almonds, blanched, slivered (10 ounces)	¾ cup	granulated sugar
		4 tablespoons	unsalted butter

Preheat the oven to 350°F.

Process all ingredients in a food processor until combined. Press evenly into the bottom and sides of a 10-inch tart pan with a removable bottom. Bake for 25 minutes or until golden brown. Set aside to cool.

FILLING

½ cup	crème frâiche (sour cream can be substituted)	¾ cup	heavy cream
		10 ounces	semi-sweet chocolate, chopped
½ cup	granulated sugar		
¾ cup	Cabernet		

In a medium saucepan bring the creme fraiche, sugar, cabernet and heavy cream to a simmer and pour over chocolate. Stir until smooth and pour into tart shell. Refrigerate at least 3 hours. Top with sugar-dusted raspberries.

Just a short 20 minute drive up Highway 59 from Houston to Humble, Chez Nous is a gem of a restaurant slightly off the beaten path. Considered one of the best French restaurants in the nation, they have operated here in a former Penecostal church, set in an unassuming neighborhood, for 25 years. Founder, Owner and Co-Executive Chef Gerard Brach originally planned to relocate to 'the city' once the restaurant was established, but fans were undaunted by the 20 minute drive and so the restaurant remains in the location to this day.

Chez Nous exudes French romance as you walk in the door. The rustic, refurbished church atmosphere adds to the French countryside ambiance and Brach's business partner and Co-Executive Chef Stacy Crowe-Simonson serves up brilliant, classic French fare on 17 different types of china, all collected by her grandmother.

The food here is classic and perfect. Select appetizers and entrees change every day but the menu is balanced with items that are favored fixtures. Chateaubriand, Foie Gras, Vichyssoise, Escargot and the succulent Rack of Lamb (carved tableside) should not be missed. Listed in Gourmet Magazine's 'America's Top Tables', Chez Nous is truly a dining experience for your gourmet 'bucket list'.

Executive Chef Randy Evans (formerly of Brennan's) promises a true farm-to-plate experience at Houston's first Certified Green Restaurant - Haven.

Evans describes the menu as 'Modern Texas Cuisine' influenced by favorite Texas food that he grew up with.

A favorite appetizer here is the shrimp corn dog served with a shot of Meyer lemonade and tabasco mash remoulade. It definitely takes you back to your childhood!

GOAT'S BUTTERMILK

1 cup	goat's milk
¼ cup	cultured buttermilk

In a clean mixing bowl combine milks and store in a clean sealed jar overnight in a warm area of the kitchen. After 24 hours the milk should be the thickness of buttermilk. Taste to make certain the buttermilk has a tart flavor, but not 'off'. Refrigerate until needed.

HAVEN
BUTTERMILK PECAN PIE

Chef Randy Evans makes his own goat's buttermilk for this pie and you can give that a shot, if you like (instructions follow). If goat's milk is not available, regular buttermilk will still make for a wonderful pie.

YIELD: 9-INCH PIE

SHELL

1¼ cups	all-purpose flour		½ cup	vegetable shortening
⅓ teaspoon	salt		3 tablespoons	ice cold water

Place the flour and salt in a large bowl; add shortening and work mixture with hands or pastry cutter just until shortening is incorporated and appears like sand for mealy dough. Add 3 tablespoons of water and mix until dough just comes together. If needed, add additional water a teaspoon at a time. Form the dough into a thick, round disc shape. Wrap in plastic wrap. Refrigerate until dough is firm.

On a lightly floured surface, evenly roll out dough from the center out to the edges until it is an even ¼-inch thick and more than large enough to cover pie tin. Use flour to dust, as needed, under and on top of dough to keep it from sticking to surface or rolling pin.

Drape the dough over the rolling pin and center it over a deep 9-inch pie dish with an edge overlapping all the way around the pan. Lightly pat dough down into pan. Fold the excess under and create desired edge by pinching with fingers or pressing with fork. Set aside.

FILLING

1 cup	pecan pieces		3	eggs, large, whisked
1¾ cups	sugar		dash	nutmeg
2 tablespoons	all-purpose flour		1¼ teaspoons	vanilla
1 cup	buttermilk		1 tablespoons	lemon juice
½ cup	unsalted butter, room temperature		pinch	salt

Preheat oven to 350˚F.

Place one cup of the pecans into the pie shell and blind bake in the oven for 5 minutes. Remove from oven and let cool on a cooling rack.

In a large mixing bowl, combine the sugar, flour and buttermilk with a whisk. Add the softened butter and mix well. Add the whisked eggs and mix well. Stir in the lemon juice and nutmeg. Pour into the blind baked pie shell. Pour into the cooled pie shell and bake for 50 to 60 minutes. Let cool. Serve with vanilla ice cream.

GOODE COMPANY
MARGARITA PIE

Goode Company's 'amped-up' rendition of a key lime pie is the ultimate summer treat. The balance is perfect - not too sweet and not too tart. The crust is a traditional graham cracker crust that adds a wonderful texture to the luscious margarita filling. Take your time and be sure to use ripe Persian limes as they are less tart than traditional limes.

YIELD: 9-INCH PIE

CRUST

1¾ cups	graham cracker crumbs		4 tablespoons	granulated sugar
½ cup	unsalted butter, (4 ounces)		pinch	salt

Preheat conventional oven to 350°F, (convection oven to 325°F).

In a small saucepan over medium heat, melt the butter until creamy but not separated.

In a medium bowl, combine the graham cracker crumbs, butter, sugar and salt and mix well.

Press into a 9-inch pie plate and bake for 15 minutes until lightly browned.

FILLING

4	egg yolks		1½ teaspoons	lime zest
1 can	sweetened condensed milk (14 ounces)		1	egg white
½ cup plus 2 tablespoons	freshly squeezed lime juice (strained)		¼ teaspoon	cream of tartar

Preheat conventional oven to 350°F (convection oven to 325°F).

Add the egg yolks to the bowl of a stand mixer with wire whisk attached. Mix for 30 seconds to break up the yolks.

Add the condensed milk and incorporate until well combined, scraping down the sides of the bowl with a spatula. Do not over mix.

Add the lime juice in a thin stream while mixing. Blend in zest until incorporated. Pour the lime mixture into a glass or plastic (non-reactive) mixing bowl.

To beat the egg whites, prepare a mixing bowl by cleaning well, and then placing in the freezer for 5 minutes. Remove from freezer.

Add the egg whites and cream of tartar the chilled bowl. Mix on medium speed, then gradually increase the speed until stiff peaks form (about 5 minutes).

Gently fold the beaten egg whites into the lime mixture.

Fill the crust and bake on the middle rack for 25 minutes or until set.

As legend has it, the Goode family restaurant dynasty began when Jim Goode wandered into a failing neighborhood barbecue 'joint' in 1977 and made a deal to purchase the establishment on the spot. With a revamped menu, they reopened just days later as Goode Company Texas Bar-B-Q. Early on, Jim and his uncle Joe Dixie spent nights at the restaurant, waking hourly to check on the slow-cooking brisket. (And they always kept a shotgun handy to protect the meat, the equipment and themselves... in that order.)

Things have changed considerably for the Goode family since their humble beginnings, but thankfully the mouth-watering food always remains a labor of love and pride. With son Levi at the helm, this family of restaurants has grown to seven, serving up some of the best barbecue, seafood, burgers and tacos in town. In 2008, Jim and Levi received a nod from the prestigious James Beard Foundation for 'Outstanding Restrateur' and were awarded an impressive 'My Table Culinary Award' as a '2009 Houston Classic'.

Opened in 1936, Brenner's Steakhouse is a legendary restaurant with a remarkable past. Originally called Brenner's Cafe, the modest eatery began as the dream of newlyweds Herman and Lorene Brenner, who paid $20 toward the purchase of the land and the construction - a small fortune painstakingly saved during a post-depression economy. Upon completion, the Brenner's moved into a small space in the back of the kitchen. They would unknowingly spend these 'lean years' perfecting a menu that would truly stand the test of time.

The original building was sold in the 1950's and the eatery was relocated to its current location. Here they would blossom, literally and figuratively - adding the now fabled gardens (a picturesque tribute to Mr. Brenner's native Germany) and becoming the toast of the newly developed Memorial Drive area. Their notoriety spread and quickly developed into national acclaim and recognition.

When the restaurant closed in 2002, Tilman Fertitta (Chairman and CEO of Landry's Restaurants, Inc.) purchased the location and revitalized the concept with the help of Lorene Brenner, who worked side-by-side with Landry's Executive Chefs to recreate its delectable menu.

BRENNER'S
APPLE STRUDEL

Although it's origin is German, this dessert is as American as baseball and Chevrolet. Old fashioned goodness abounds with a filling of caramelized Granny Smith apples spiced with cinnamon, rum and crunchy toasted pecans rolled in a flaky golden brown crust. Be sure to use a linen napkin to roll out the puff pastry dough - it's critical to being able to roll the strudel up properly so it is tight and even.

YIELD: ONE STRUDEL, 8 SERVINGS

FILLING

1 cup	unsalted butter		6	apples, peeled, cored, and sliced (2½ pounds)
1¼ pounds	brown sugar			
2 teaspoons	ground cinnamon			
2 teaspoons	fresh lemon juice		¼ cup	cornstarch
3 tablespoons	Meyers rum		⅓ cup	cold water

In an extra large skillet, melt the butter over medium heat.

Add the brown sugar, cinnamon, lemon juice and rum. Whisk until completely incorporated.

Add the apples to the sugar mixture and cook over medium heat until cooked through, approximately 20 minutes. Combine the cornstarch and water and add to skillet. Cook until mixture thickens and then turn off heat. Transfer to an appropriate storage container. Cool in an ice bath.

Place the cooled strudel filling into a perforated pan and allow most of the juices drain (you mainly want apples inside the strudel to keep it crisp).

ASSEMBLY

1 batch	apple strudel filling		as needed	all-purpose flour
1 each	puff pastry sheets, thawed			water
				egg wash
¼ cup	toasted pecans			

Place a linen napkin down on a work table. Dust the napkin with flour and place puff pastry on the floured napkin. Roll out to twice its original size (about the size of the napkin).

Place the strudel filling it the center third of the puff pastry, then sprinkle ¼ cup of pecans on top. Fold one end of pastry over the filling (using the linen napkin to fold it), brush with water, fold over the other end, and gently press together.

Pinch excess pastry from the ends and fold the ends over the top (all seams should be on the same side). Flip so the seam is on the bottom. Place the strudel on a parchment lined sheet pan and brush with egg wash. Cover and freeze for at least 12 hours.

Preheat convection oven to 375°F (regular oven 400°F).

Remove the strudel from the freezer and place on a sheet pan lined with parchment paper. Brush again with egg wash.

Bake frozen strudel until golden brown on the outside, approximately 20 minutes. Slice each strudel into 8 equal pieces, discarding a 1-inch piece on each end. Serve with vanilla ice cream.

COOKIES,
ICE CREAM & CANDY

Biscuits, keks, galletas, biscottis, amarettis or cookies, regardless the name, they are a nostalgic treat that has not a single detractor. Everybody likes cookies.

In most languages, the word 'cookie' translates roughly to 'small cake', which also explains their origin. Early bakers would often use a small amount of cake batter to test the heat of the oven and the resulting 'little cake' caught on.

When making cookies, these tips might come in handy:

-Lighter cookie sheets with low or no sides are best. Dull finishes encourage even browning. Shiny finishes will retard browning - perfect for sugar and shortbread cookies.

-Cookie dough logs can be frozen for up to 1 month, which is great if you just want to bake a small batch. Slice the dough while frozen and bake as directed.

You would think that ice cream would have to wait to be discovered until refrigeration was invented, but the Chinese were mixing cream and ice as far back as 618 A.D. Perhaps the greatest discovery was lowering the temperature of the ice by adding salt and incorporating the rotating paddle - an invention patented by Nancy Johnson in 1846. It remains the basic method for ice cream production to this day.

When making ice creams and gelatos, consider these helpful tips:

-Ideally, churn-frozen ice cream is best if you make the mixture and chill it in the refrigerator the day before you freeze. This will increase the yield and help create smooth texture and a well incorporated flavor.

-The faster the freeze, the smoother the texture will be.

-Ice cream is best stored between -5 and 0˚F.

Pappas' Greek Kitchen, Yia Yia Mary's, offers a selection of unique and flavorful cuisine from the Mediterranean.

Grilled chicken, beef and shrimp kabobs, flavorful Greek breads and a variety of select appetizers, including hummus and baked cheeses, provide something for everyone.

NOTE: Clarified butter is pure liquid gold butterfat. Also know as drawn butter or ghee, clarified butter is unsalted butter that has had the milk solids and water removed. It has an incredibly high smoking point and lasts for months in the refrigerator.

CLARIFIED BUTTER Melt unsalted butter in a large stockpot over low heat. Turn off the heat when the butter is fully melted. Let cool. Skim the milk solids off the top and pour the rest through a fine meshed sieve if using right away...or refrigerate the stockpot for a few hours or overnight. Once chilled, you can easily remove the block of clarified butter off the top of the water. The next day skim the milk solids off the top and remove the block of clarified butter off the top of the water.

TIP: Although I am not sure how healthful, the milk solids that you skim off the top are delicious poured over popcorn with a little fresh parmesan grated on top.

YIA YIA MARY'S
KOURAMBIEDES

Two things are guaranteed at any Greek family celebration: ouzo and Kourambiedes.

These celebratory cookies are often as unique as the family that makes them. Kourambiedes recipes have been handed down for generations and spices and ingredients vary widely.

Yia Yia Mary's Kourambiedes recipe comes from Yia Yia Mary herself and was passed down to her from her own yia yia (Greek for grandmother). It yields a traditional almond shortbread cookie with a delightful buttery texture, complete with a heaving dusting of powdered sugar. These classic cookies have a delectable, melt-in-your-mouth quality that just might inspire you to pass Yia Yia Mary's recipe along in your own family.

YIELD: 30 COOKIES

2 cups plus 6 tablespoons	clarified butter, softened (19 ounces)	¼ teaspoon	almond extract
6 tablespoons	granulated sugar	1 tablespoon	lemon juice
¼ cup	whiskey	½ tablespoon	baking soda
⅓ teaspoon	rose water	4½ cups	all-purpose flour
¼ teaspoon	vanilla extract	¾ cup	almonds, sliced and slightly crushed by hand
		for dusting	powdered sugar

Preheat oven to 300°F.

In the bowl of a stand mixer with paddle attachment, cream butter and sugar until light and fluffy, about 10 to 15 minutes.

Stop and scrape the sides and bottom of the bowl occasionally.

In a mixing bowl, combine whiskey, rosewater, vanilla extract, almond extract, lemon juice, and baking soda and whisk until baking soda is dissolved.

Add the whiskey mixture to the creamed butter and mix on low speed until just combined.

Add the flour and almonds to the mixer and mix on medium speed for 2 minutes. Stop and scrape the sides and bottom of the bowl to ensure that ingredients are evenly distributed throughout the dough. Mix on medium speed for an additional 2 minutes.

Portion dough into golf ball-sized balls and place on baking sheet. Press each down slightly with the palm of your hand.

Bake for 15 minutes, rotate tray, then bake for an additional 15 minutes.

Remove from the oven and allow to cool for 5 minutes.

Finish the cookies by dusting generously with powdered sugar.

REBECCA MASSON
FLUFFERNUTTERS

Inspired by her childhood affinity for Fluffernutter sandwiches and Nutter Butter cookies, Rebecca was determined to perfect this cookie. She tested every available brand of peanut butter and discovered that good old Skippy gets the job done best. The end result - the most perfect peanut butter cookies you've ever tasted, sandwiched around a sugary peanut butter filling and a dollop of marshmallow fluff.

Warning! They are addictive! (But, I can't think of a more heavenly habit.)

YIELD: 24 COOKIES

COOKIES

1 cup	unsalted butter, softened (8 ounces)		2 cups	peanut butter
2 cups	brown sugar		2 cups	all-purpose flour
3	eggs		2 cups	old fashioned oats
2 teaspoons	vanilla extract		1 teaspoon	baking soda
			½ teaspoon	salt

Preheat oven to 350°F.

In a stand mixer, cream the butter and sugar - this process should take 5 to 10 minutes.

Add the eggs one at time, until well combined. Then add the vanilla and peanut butter and mix well.

Next, add the dry ingredients, a little at a time, mixing well.

Scoop ¾ ounce spoonfuls onto a baking sheet. Bake for 10 to 12 minutes.

Press cookies down with your palm to flatten when they come out of oven.

FILLING

1 cup	peanut butter		1 cup	powdered sugar
½ cup	unsalted butter (4 ounces)		1 jar	marshmallow fluff (packaged)

In a stand mixer, combine the peanut butter, the butter and sugar and cream until smooth.

Spoon the peanut butter filling and marshmallow fluff into two separate pastry bags or ziploc bags with a corner cut off. Once the cookies have cooled, pipe a circle of the peanut butter filling on the flat side of a cookie and put a blob of marshmallow fluff in the middle of the circle. Sandwich together.

Known by many as the 'Sugar Hooker of Houston', Rebecca Masson's confectionery 'wares' grace many a well-known Houston kitchen. Trained at France's Le Cordon Bleu, Rebecca first worked as Pastry Chef for The Red Cat in Manhattan before returning to Texas. Houstonians can thankfully get their 'fix' of her delightful creations at top restaurants like *17 at the Alden, Ibiza, Catalan and Bailey's.

The retro accent of her creations are featured multiple times in this book. Check out Ibiza's Lemon Meringue tart (a tribute to her great grandmother) and the sundae of all sundaes, Stella Sola's Caramel Turtle Affogato. Try them all. You will find that her recipes produce old-fashioned flavors that appeal to virtually everyone.

Masson was named Pastry Chef of the Year in My Table magazine's 2007 Annual Awards for Culinary Excellence and her inventive recipes have been featured in Time Magazine, New York Daily News and on CNN, who recognized her as being a chocolate expert.

The simple name belies a vast amount of experience going on behind the scenes at Mo's - A Place for Steaks. With locations in Milwaukee, Indianapolis, and Houston, owner John A. Vassallo has cemented Mo's as an upscale dining establishment renowned for its sumptuously prepared top-quality beef and welcoming social scene.

Highly acclaimed Chef Eric Aldis began his career at the Four Seasons Hotel in Houston and went on to such notable eateries as the Ritz-Carlton New Orleans, Bellagio and Melange. He is now happily ensconced in the kitchen and front of the house at Mo's and Houston 'foodies' couldn't be happier.

Offering their famous tableside presentation of premium steaks and chops, Mo's also offers a wide selection of over 300 international and domestic wines as well as award-winning appetizers and desserts, a piano bar and a heated/air-conditioned patio for comfortable al fresco dining.

MO'S - A PLACE FOR STEAKS
HALF-BAKED CHOCOLATE CHIP COOKIE

The half-baked chocolate chips cookies are served family style at Mo's so everyone can get in on the action. This huge, gooey chocolate chip cookie, ice cream and chocolate sauce combination makes for an even more memorable evening.

Remember this is a half-baked treat - don't overcook!

YIELD: 6 COOKIES

¾ cup	granulated sugar
¾ cup	packed brown sugar
1 cup	unsalted butter, softened (8 ounces)
1 teaspoon	vanilla extract
2	large eggs, beaten

2¼ cups	all-purpose flour
1 teaspoon	baking soda
¾ teaspoon	salt
2 cups	semi-sweet chocolate chips

Preheat oven to 375˚F.

In a stand mixer with paddle attachment on a low speed, mix the sugar, brown sugar, butter, vanilla and eggs.

In a separate bowl, combine the flour, baking soda and salt and stir to combine.

Add the dry mixture, a little bit at time, making sure to mix well. Scrape down the sides and bottom of the bowl to make sure the dough is mixed well.

Using a sturdy wooden spoon and a bit of muscle, stir in the chocolate chips. Keep stirring and fold the chocolate chips into the dough until they are evenly dispersed.

Press 8 ounces of cookie dough into the bottom of a 6 to 8-ounce oven safe dish.

Bake 6 to 10 minutes until light brown.

Top with vanilla ice cream and chocolate sauce.

Vincent and Mary Mandola have been delivering the essence of Italy's food and ambiance at their flagship restaurant, Nino's, for over 32 years.

The eye-catching, colorful array of marinated and baked vegetables makes you want to pull up a chair and sit down...right there at the 18th century antipasto table. Only the finest and freshest ingredients are used in their veal, seafood, chicken and pasta dishes. Their house specialty, my personal favorite, is the Pollo Arrosto- lemon-garlic rotisserie chicken. It is the most amazing bird you have ever tasted. The veal picatta is a favorite of my husband's.

Just steps from Nino's are Vincent's and Grappino de Nino-the Mandola's Italian grappa bar.

And, if you have a taste for that chicken but don't want to go out for dinner proper, you can easily get it from their take-out restaurant, Pronto Cucinino!

FRESH SAUTEED ORANGE PEEL

½	orange
3½ tablespoons	granulated sugar
1½ tablespoons	orange liqueur

Cut the orange in half, then cut into ¼-inch slices. Remove fruit from the rind and reserve for another use. In a large saute pan over medium high heat, combine the orange rind slices, sugar and orange liqueur, stirring constantly, until the liquid is reduced to a syrup. Remove from heat and let cool to room temperature. Store in an air tight container in the refrigerator. Chop orange peel as needed.

NINO'S
CANNOLI

Remember the famous quote from the movie 'The Godfather', "Forget the guns! Take t cannoli!"? Well, Nino's cannoli is just that good! These delectably crunchy pastry tubes are fill with velvety satin ricotta cheese, mini chocolate chips and fresh sauteed orange peel. The smal size of these cannoli leaves little room for guilt.

YIELD: 6 SERVINGS

SHELLS

2 teaspoons	granulated sugar		¼ teaspoon	vegetable oil
7 tablespoons	all-purpose flour		2 teaspoons	egg, beaten
½ teaspoon	nutmeg		2 teaspoons	water
¼ teaspoon	cinnamon		¼ teaspoon	salt
¼ teaspoon	baking powder		3 tablespoons	Lambrusco (or other red wine)

In a large bowl, add sugar, flour, nutmeg, cinnamon, salt and baking powder. Mix well. Add t vegetable oil and egg, and mix again. Add the Lambrusco and mix well. Dough should be stick Spread out plastic film and put flour on the film. Take the dough and roll it on the floured plas film. Let rest for 30 minutes.

On a floured surface, roll out the dough to ⅛-inch thick. Cut sheets of dough into into 4-in circles. Layer each piece of dough on a floured sheet pan. Be sure to sprinkle extra flour in betwe each piece of dough as you layer. This should be enough for 12 shells.

Roll each piece of dough around a cannoli shell tube and seal the end of the dough with a drop water. Pour 3 to 4-inches of oil into a deep skillet or Dutch oven and heat to 350˚F.

Carefully place each tube into the hot oil, and fry until golden brown. Drain well on paper towe remove the tube and store in a covered container.

FILLING

1 tub	ricotta cheese (15 ounces)		2 tablespoons	fresh sauteed orange peel, chopped
2 tablespoons	powdered sugar			
2 tablespoons	mini chocolate chips			

In a medium mixing bowl, beat the ricotta cheese and powdered sugar together until silky smoo but be careful not to over mix. Fold in the chocolate chips and orange peel. Refrigerate in covered container.

Put the cannoli filling into a pastry bag or ziploc bag with a corner snipped off. Fill each side of t cannoli with filling. Dip each end in chopped pistachios.

RUSTIKA CAFE
ALFAJOR

Alfajores (al-fa-hor-es) are a delightful Spanish shortbread sandwich cookie with a dulce de leche (caramel) filling. Spanish conquest brought the cookie to Latin America where it flourished and was refined, most notably in Argentina where it reigns as a signature dessert. These cookies are both rustic and fancy, a perfect lighter ending after a heavy meal.

YIELD: 12 TO 24 COOKIES

¾ cup	cornstarch
½ cup	all-purpose flour
½ teaspoon	baking powder
½ cup	unsalted butter, softened (4 ounces)
⅔ cup	granulated sugar
3	egg yolks
½ teaspoon	vanilla extract
1 jar	dulce de leche (packaged)
as needed	chocolate frosting

Preheat the oven to 350°F.

In a small bowl, whisk together the cornstarch, flour and baking powder. Set aside.

In the bowl of an electric mixer fitted with the paddle attachment, beat the egg yolks well, add sugar and continue to beat. Then add softened butter and vanilla and continue to beat.

Working in batches, add the flour mixture and mix until well combined, forming dough. Add a couple of drops of water, if necessary, to make a pliable dough.

Roll the dough out to about ½-inch thick. Using a 2-inch round cookie cutter, cut circles from the dough.

Place the cookies onto a greased or parchment lined cookie sheet or pan.

Transfer to the oven and bake for 20 minutes, rotating the baking sheet halfway through cooking.

The bottom should be golden brown but the top should still be white.

Spread the dulce de leche on the brown side of the cookies. Sandwich the 2 cookies together, dulce side in, and spread a little more dulce de leche around the edges of the cookies. Then roll the borders through nuts or grated coconut. You can then frost one or both sides of the cookie with chocolate or white chocolate frosting.

These cookies are at their best the following day.

Rustika Cafe & Bakery offers a surprising hybrid of Mexican and Jewish creations that are always in great demand. Rare is the restaurant that offers fresh-baked empanadas, migas and chilaquiles alongside blintzes, matzoh ball soup and what are apparently the hottest jalapeno gefelte fish you've ever tasted.

Mexico City native Francis Reznick and her artistic bakers are known for their amazing cake creations, but the food they offer at their storefront is the real star. Stellar soups, oversized sandwiches and savory empanadas are among the preferred items here, as are amazing breakfast items and coffees. And then of course, there is the dessert menu. Good luck choosing between Mexican danishes with cream cheese, apricot and raspberry preserves, fresh baked empanadas filled with pumpkin and sprinkled with cinnamon or artisan cookies: lemon cornmeal, almond butter or Mexican wedding. We find it's easier to just order it all and take it home to enjoy at your leisure.

CARAMEL SAUCE

1¼ cups	granulated sugar
3 tablespoons	water
3 tablespoons	light Karo syrup
½ teaspoon	fresh lemon juice
1 cup	heavy cream

Combine the granulated sugar, water, light Karo syrup, and lemon juice in a saucepot over medium heat. Bring just up to a boil then lower heat. Simmer until caramel turns medium brown to amber in color. Remove from heat and very slowly whisk in heavy cream (whisking too fast will cause the caramel to overflow).

Pour into container with lid and allow to cool.

CHOCOLATE SAUCE

½ cup plus 1 tablespoon	unsalted butter (4½ ounces)
6 tablespoons	water
4 ounces	semi-sweet chocolate chips
½ cup	granulated sugar
2½ tablespoons	light Karo syrup
¾ teaspoon	vanilla extract

Combine the unsalted butter and water in a saucepot over medium heat. Once the butter has melted, add the chocolate chips, sugar, and light Karo syrup. Bring up to a boil, stirring to thoroughly incorporate. Reduce the heat and simmer until chocolate is smooth. Remove from heat and stir in vanilla extract. Strain through a fine mesh sieve and allow to cool.

PAPPAS BROS. STEAKHOUSE
MACADAMIA NUT BLONDE BROWNIE

Blondies or brownies? It's the age-old dessert dilemma. That is, unless you're at Pappas Brothers Steakhouse, where the Macadamia Nut Blonde Brownie pairs the rich and buttery flavor of a blondie with luscious chocolate chips and crunchy macadamia nuts. For added decadence, just before serving, heat brownie in the oven for five minutes, then top with a scoop of ice cream.

It's the best of both worlds and out of this one!

YIELD: 12 TO 15 SERVINGS

1¼ cups	semi-sweet chocolate chunks
¾ cup	toasted macadamia nuts, whole
1 pound	dark brown sugar
½ cup plus 2 tablespoons	unsalted butter, melted and hot (5 ounces)
2½ tablespoons	vanilla extract
2	eggs
2 cups	all-purpose flour
1½ teaspoons	baking powder
½ teaspoon	salt
	caramel sauce
	chocolate sauce

Preheat oven to 275° F.

Spray a 9-by-13-inch pan with nonstick spray. Then line the pan with parchment paper.

In a food processor, pulse the chocolate chunks and macadamia nuts until coarsely ground.

Place the dark brown sugar and hot melted butter in the bowl of a stand mixer with a paddle attachment. Mix on medium speed for 5 minutes. Drizzle in extracts and add in eggs one at a time. Once all of the eggs have been added, stop the mixer and scrape the sides and bottom of the bowl. Return mixer to medium speed and continue mixing for 5 minutes.

In a separate bowl, sift flour, baking powder, and salt together. Turn mixer to low and slowly add sifted ingredients. Mix for 10 seconds, stop and scrape the sides and bottom of the bowl.

Continue to mix on low for 2 more minutes. Add the chocolate/macadamia nut mixture and mix for 20 seconds, or until nuts and chocolate are dispersed throughout the batter.

Pour batter into the prepared pan and bake for 40 to 45 minutes, or until a cake tester comes out clean.

Cool to room temperature.

Once completely cooled you can cut either square or circular brownies. Place in the center of the dish and top with scoop of ice cream. Drizzle with caramel sauce and chocolate sauce.

MOLINA'S
PECAN PRALINES

Pray-leen or prah-leen, pee-kahn or pee-can? No matter how you say it, this southern delicacy should be the official candy of Texas!

The French were the first to make pralines using almonds and caramelized sugar, the Tex-Mex have made them their own by using pecans.

If you want to be fancy, put half of a pecan on top of each praline.

YIELD: 2 DOZEN

2⅓ cups	milk	4 cups	sugar
1¾ teaspoons	vanilla	1 cup	pecan pieces
pinch	cinnamon		

In a heavy bottomed sauce pan over medium heat, combine the milk, vanilla, cinnamon and sugar. Stir frequently to avoid sticking and burning. If mixture burns, scorches or sticks, you must start over. Cook until the thermometer reaches 235-240°F, the soft ball stage. This is a long process. You will need to boil mixture for 45 minutes to 1 hour.

To test, remove the pot from the heat (so it does not scorch) and drop a small spoonful into cold water. The candy should form a soft, loose ball. If this stage has not been reached, return the pot to the heat.

Add pecan pieces and pour candy into small sauté pan. Stir until it thickens slightly and spoon about 2 tablespoons onto waxed paper to let cool.

Store in a tightly covered container or wrap individually.

NOTE: Using a cast iron pot will yield the best results. In case you are unaware, cast iron pots and skillets, even the most unattractive, rusted ones, can be incredibly valuable. My mother-in-law just happens to be a cast iron skillet aficionado. As such, she has quite a collection. I have been the fortunate recipient of many and treasure each and every one of them.

CAUTION: Boiling sugar is very dangerous and extremely painful. Please take care.

In 1929, when Raul Molina came to Houston from Laredo to seek a better life, he had no idea he would play such an integral role in the future of Houston's culinary landscape.

He started as a dishwasher and busboy at Old Monterrey Restaurant and 10 years later he bought the place. The whole family not only worked and ate there, they lived in one room above the restaurant. Lots of love and determination made the family business a success.

After two years as restaurateurs, Raul and his wife bought another restaurant, the Mexico City restaurant. While their sons were away serving their country, they were made partners in the business. In 1952 the restaurant was renamed Molina's Mexico City Restaurant and eventually became Molina's Restaurant & Cantina.

More restaurants have been opened and relocated following Houston's changing demographic and growth. The term mi familia encompasses not only family members but also employees and customers. Some of their employees have been with them for 30 years and customers who grew up with Molina's family now bring their children and grandchildren to the restaurant. Today, Raul, Jr.'s three sons own and operate the restaurants.

The Molina's tradition has been carried on for generations and is bound by corazon, "the heart of Molina's".

Texas meets Tuscany? It's a winning if not surprising combination. Stella Sola (Italian for 'Lone Star') features cuisine combining Texas culture and ingredients with the flavors and influences of northern Italy.

Stella Sola's kitchen makes everything in-house including sausages, cheeses and fresh pastas. They even dry age their own cuts of meat, a feature of the very popular and much lauded Charcuterie Platter by Chef de Cuisine Justin Basye. The menu also includes flat breads, slow braised meat dishes and fresh catches from the Gulf.

CANDIED PECANS

½ cup	corn syrup
1 cup	pecan halves
¼ teaspoon	salt
¼ teaspoon	cinnamon

Toss everything together in a bowl until completely covered. Lay out on a sheet pan lined with a sil-pat or parchment paper. Cook at 325° F for about 12 minutes, until syrup begins to bubble. When the coating hardens, carefully remove nuts from pan and place in a bowl. Stir the nuts until they cool down and break apart. Store in an airtight container.

STELLA SOLA
CARAMEL TURTLE AFFOGATO

At Stella Sola, the theme is Texas-Tuscan. This one dessert manages to tie in both of those themes. Affogato is a traditional Italian espresso-based dessert and the 'turtle' flavors represent the Texas side of the dish. This Rebecca Masson creation has it all. It's hot, cold, salty, sweet, crunchy and gooey. Salted caramel ice cream, drizzled with espresso chocolate and laced with candied pecans, it just doesn't get any better than this! Be sure to use gray sea salt for the ice cream - it really makes a difference.

YIELD: 6 SERVINGS

SALTED CARAMEL ICE CREAM

10	egg yolks		¼ cup	water
pinch	gray sea salt		2 cups	milk
1 cup	granulated sugar		2 cups	heavy cream

In a bowl, whisk egg yolks with kosher salt; set aside.

In a heavy saucepan, stir together the sugar and the water and cook over medium heat, stirring occasionally, until sugar has dissolved. Increase the heat to high and cook, without stirring, until sugar is dark amber in color.

Meanwhile, combine the milk and the heavy cream in saucepan. Bring to a simmer and remove from heat.

Slowly pour cream mixture into sugar mixture, using extreme caution. Stir to combine. Bring the caramel back to a boil, making sure all the caramel has dissolved, then remove from heat.

Slowly pour one cup of the caramel cream mixture into the eggs, whisking as you pour. Slowly pour the egg yolk mixture into remaining caramel cream, continuing to whisk while you pour. Return custard to stove and cook over low heat, stirring with a wooden spoon until mixture is thick enough to lightly coat the back of the spoon, about 7 minutes.

Remove from heat, pour mixture through a fine sieve and chill at least 4 hours, preferably overnight. Freeze mixture in ice cream machine, following manufacturer's instructions.

To assemble sundae, scoop ice cream into a glass, drizzle with the chocolate espresso sauce and top with the candied pecans.

CHOCOLATE ESPRESSO SAUCE

1 cup	water		18 ounces	semi-sweet chocolate, coarsely chopped
1⅔ cups	granulated sugar			
⅔ cup	light corn syrup		3 tablespoons	brewed, strong espresso
½ cup	cocoa powder		1 pinch	salt

Bring the water, sugar and corn syrup to a boil in a large saucepan. Once boiling, stir in the cocoa powder. Return to a boil and then remove from heat. Pour over the chocolate and stir until combined. Add espresso and salt. Let cool. You will have plenty left over but it is wonderful!

COCONUT ALMOND JOY

As a teenager, my grandma Patsy's favorite thing to do every day after school was to stop by the store to get an Almond Joy candy bar and a Coke. For her, this recipe brought all of those memories flooding back.

YIELD: 1½ QUARTS

1⅓ cups	milk	½ cup	raw, unsalted, chopped almonds
¾ cup	granulated sugar	½ cup	bittersweet chocolate, finely chopped
3 cups	half-and-half	1 tablespoon	vegetable oil
⅔ cup	non-fat powdered milk	½ cup	Coconut Almond Joy candy chopped into small pieces
⅓ cup	light corn syrup		
¾ cup	coconut milk		
⅔ cup	cream of coconut	3 bars	Coconut Almond Joy candy (6 pieces)
½ cup	unsweetened shredded coconut		
½ teaspoon	vanilla extract		

In a heavy saucepan, combine the milk, sugar, powdered milk, and corn syrup, and bring to approximately 155–175° F. Use an electric hand held mixer as it heats to prevent burning or sticking. Whisk until the sugar and powdered milk have dissolved and the mixture had reached the desired temperature. Remove from the heat and allow to cool. After the mixture has cooled, place in the refrigerator overnight.

Remove the gelato base from the refrigerator, set aside.

In a blender, combine the shredded coconut, coconut milk, cream of coconut and vanilla extract. Blend until completely mixed and almost smooth. There should still be some smaller, visible pieces of shredded coconut. Set aside.

Mix the gelato base with the blended coconut mixture and put into the ice cream freezer. Freeze per the manufacturer's directions.

Chop the almonds into small pieces. Set aside in a small bowl.

In a small microwave-safe bowl, combine the chocolate and oil. Heat on low heat, stirring about every 15 seconds, until the chocolate is melted and the oil is completely combined with the chocolate. Alternatively, warm the chocolate in a heat-proof bowl over a saucepan of simmering water for about 2 minutes. Turn off the heat but keep on the stove to keep warm.

Just as the gelato is ready, but before it is too firm to manage, fold in the chopped almonds and candy. Drizzle the melted chocolate over the gelato, using a spatula, spoon or a squirt bottle. The chocolate will freeze hard upon hitting the gelato. Using a squirt bottle is the easiest method.

Return the gelato to the freezer for at least 2 hours before serving.

Garnish each serving with one small bar of Coconut Almond Joy Candy, either whole or cut in half.

Chef Chuck Irwin loves all things Italian, specifically gelato, which he first tasted in Italy. The Italian gelateria is an important part of daily life where friends gather to socialize and enjoy a treat. He has recreated that experience with his gelato.

Gelato Blu is an authentic Italian gelato made in the strictest Italian standards. All the gelati and sorbetti are made from scratch with both local and Italian imported ingredients. Gelato Blu gelato can be found in many restaurants and coffee shops. The flavor list here now tops over 100. Customer favorites include 'Michelangelo', a complex gelato with hints of ricotta cheese and fig and 'Orange Push-Up', the flavor we all know and love from childhood.

In addition to some of the best handmade gelato Houston has to offer, Chef Chuck Irwin also exclusively imports Manuel Coffee, a remarkable, Italian imported coffee and espresso blend produced by a privately held third generation coffee roaster.

Keeping true to the Pappas tradition of freshness, all sauces, marinades, guacamole, salad dressings and even the delectable homemade tortillas are made from scratch. The only thing that comes frozen at Pappasito's is their fabulous margarita, made with fresh lime juice for an added zing!

CHOCOLATE SAUCE

½ cup plus 1 tablespoon	unsalted butter
6 tablespoons	water
4 ounces	semi-sweet chocolate chips
½ cup	granulated sugar
2½ tablespoons	light Karo syrup
¾ teaspoon	vanilla extract

Combine the unsalted butter and water in a saucepot over medium heat. Once the butter has melted, add the chocolate chips, sugar, and light Karo syrup. Bring up to a boil, stirring to thoroughly incorporate.

Reduce the heat to low and simmer until the chocolate is smooth. Remove from the heat and stir in the vanilla extract.

Strain the chocolate sauce through a fine mesh sieve and allow to cool.

WHIPPED CREAM

1 cup	heavy cream
¼ cup	granulated sugar

Whisk the heavy cream and granulated sugar in a mixing bowl until the cream holds stiff peaks. Store in refrigerator until needed.

PAPPASITO'S
CAJETA

For decades, Houstonians have been enjoying Pappasito's Cajeta- a huge scoop of ice cream, crusted in toasted coconut and pecans, then drenched in velvety caramel and rich chocolate sauce. This recipe is simple and delicious and the messiness is easily remedied with a little bit of finger-licking.

When making this dessert for a large group, form the ice cream balls and coat with the toasted coconut and pecan topping ahead of time. Store on a sheet tray lined with plastic wrap in the freezer until needed. When it's time for serving, simply remove the balls from the freezer, place them on plates, and drizzle with caramel and chocolate sauce.

YIELD: 2 SERVINGS

2 cups	ice cream		3 tablespoons	caramel sauce
⅓ cup	toasted coconut & pecan coating		1 tablespoon	chocolate sauce
			1 tablespoon	whipped cream

For each serving, take the ice cream directly from freezer and scoop into a large ball. Roll the ball in the toasted coconut and pecan pieces, covering the ice cream entirely.

Set in the center of the plate and pour 3 tablespoons caramel sauce directly on top.

Drizzle 1 tablespoon chocolate sauce on and around the ball. Garnish with whipped cream, strawberry, mint, and lightly dust with cinnamon.

TOASTED COCONUT & PECAN COATING

2½ cups	coconut, sweetened		1 cup	pecan pieces, medium sized

Preheat oven to 350°F.

Place the coconut and pecan pieces on a metal sheet pan. Toast until golden brown, stirring mixture occasionally to ensure even browning. Remove from oven and allow to cool on sheet pan. Once completely cooled, place in a large mixing bowl.

CARAMEL SAUCE

1¼ cups	granulated sugar		½ teaspoon	lemon juice, fresh
3 tablespoons	water		1 cup	heavy cream
3 tablespoons	light Karo syrup			

Combine the granulated sugar, water, light Karo syrup, and lemon juice in a saucepot over medium heat.

Bring just up to a boil then lower heat. Simmer until caramel turns medium brown to amber in color.

Remove from heat and very slowly whisk in the heavy cream (whisking too fast will cause the caramel to overflow). Pour into container with lid and allow to cool.

Index

ACKNOWLEDGMENTS

One never really knows how a dessert will turn out until it's made and tasted. My love of cooking and baking comes from both of my wonderful grandmothers who happily encouraged me to help them when I was a child. Sweet memories.

I owe a debt of gratitude to the many people who made this book possible.

I am forever indebted to my husband, William Jones Miller, one of the most talented people I know, whose awesome photography and production know-how brought this book to life. I'm especially grateful to Kit Wohl, an incredible woman who provided not only opportunity but inspiration, knowledge and encouragement. Jeffrey Linthicum, my wonderful editor, forever cleverly articulate and knew what I meant, even when I did not. Bob Patterson, my invaluable counsel, who always has my back. Lorie James, my friend who coined the phrase 'blow-your-skirt-up-good' which became the standard on which recipes were chosen. Georgia Epperson of Gourmet & Gadgets, need I say more? Alton Brown and Ina Garten: without lessons from their shows, I would have been a lost cowgirl. And thank you, thank you, to the great team at Pelican Publishing.

Bouquets to all of my recipe testers, especially: Leigh Williams, Christy Breining, Barbara With, Janice Gray, Sharon Sedwick, Lori Dixon, Alana Seal and Molly Merkle. Some of you tested and retested and tested again. Recipe tasters were plentiful and some gladly did double duty. Bless you all.

I own up to any errors, and encourage you to contact my publisher regarding any you may find.

And finally, my sincere appreciation to all of the chefs, pastry chefs and restaurants that contributed not only their recipes but also their patience when I was testing their recipes. Without their time, effort and talent there would be far fewer sweet endings.